OPENING YOUR PRESENCE

Presenting the YOU
You Want Others to See

GRETA MULLER

Marie Street Press

Opening Your Presence

Cover design and illustrations by
Roberta M. Granzen

ISBN: 978-0-9854148-5-6

First Printing: 2014

MARIE STREET PRESS
5760 Legacy Drive, Suite B3-454
Plano, TX 75024

Tel +1 214.519.8033

http://mariestreetpress.com

*This book is dedicated to
anyone wanting to be heard.*

Greta has a depth of experience and the unique ability to quickly meet people "where they are at." Her laser focus on issues provides meaningful insights and actionable guidance for successful outcomes. *Opening Your Presence* is the next best thing to being with Greta personally.

Catherine Burnett,
Group Director, Strategy at Pathway Group LLC

Great present! How nice to think you know it all and then get a gift of new knowledge. What a joy to learn more from a trusted resource like Greta Muller who provides a current, thoughtful approach to presence in the communication arena.

Carol Anderson,
Anderson Communications

For years, only industry insiders and clients have been able to benefit from Greta's wealth of knowledge and experience. I'm so glad she is now sharing her presents and presence with so many more! No matter what audience you are hoping to connect with, Greta's guidance can help you unlock tools you had no idea you even possessed.

Jennifer Abney,
Award-winning Anchor and Reporter

I have known Greta Muller personally and professionally for more than 20 years. I admired her work as a professional actress on stage and screen and then have called upon her for advice as an actor and now as a professional in the non-profit arena. Greta's years of experience as a communicator and a self-actualized human being give her a unique ability: to translate how one can transcend one's own baggage to engage those around them with one's authentic self.

Melissa Cameron,
Chief Development Officer,
Dallas Area Habitat for Humanity

Greta Muller is *the* source! For anyone needing to take his or her communication skills up a notch (or, better yet, to the top) then *Opening Your Presence* is the book for you. Ms. Muller hits the message out of the park, immediately connecting with her audience. Read this book; think about it; practice it—this person knows her field.

Phillip Sprayberry, DLitt,
William Paterson University

Greta has captured what it feels like to be the person who has knowledge and skills, but doesn't trust themselves to share in a presentational setting. Her insight is rare, and valuable.

Lynn Gartley,
Executive Vice President, Coaching Services
Talent Dynamics

Greta was the first consultant I ever met with in my first on-air job as a news anchor and reporter. I'll never forget our many meetings and how she helped me build my confidence. All these years later, I'm still learning from Greta through her new book. In *Opening Your Presence*, Greta lays out a road map to help you stop and think so you can achieve any goal. A great read!

Shelley Brown,
Anchor, WVUE

Opening Your Presence has something for everyone. Whether you are an aspiring young professional or a seasoned corporate executive, Greta takes the simple yet profound concept of 'authentic self' to a place which allows us a fresh perspective of ourselves. Guiding us every step of the way, Greta's journey through clarity to empowerment is both uncomplicated and refreshing.

Charles Gremillion,
Sr. Director Brand Performance Support,
Curio, Hilton Worldwide

Being able to deliver one's message as intended is an invaluable tool. Ms. Muller is a gifted coach and writer-through her personal experiences, sense of humor and guided steps; she provides the means to sharpen this tool while helping the reader feel comfortable in the fact that "I am not alone in this."

Lisa Mendelson,
Managing Director, TRB Advisors

It is not often that someone writes about talking and still captures the emotion, humor and frustrations that go into crafting the right message. I particularly appreciate that Greta's insights are designed to develop trust in oneself. As a restaurateur, I can appreciate being responsible for the bottom line. I also often find myself in the public eye and my work with Greta as well as *Opening Your Presence* was beneficial to boosting my confidence in presenting my genuine persona.

Lynae Fearing,
Co-Owner, Shinsei

Table of Contents

Foreword

Congratulations on making an important investment toward your success. *Opening Your Presence* provides some outstanding and practical insights on how to better influence others and help ensure that you are doing all you can to deliver a winning message.

Growing up the son of a hotelier, I was around the hospitality industry all of my life. At 14 years old, my Dad started work as a bellman to support his family and luckily he landed in a field that he found out was in his blood.

Dad never pushed me to follow in his footsteps, but I guess I have that same blood, because I too chose this business. My childhood goal to be just like my Dad was realized.

In my business I quickly learned that knowing your customer, genuinely demonstrating you care for them and then delivering on a promise were the foundations for building strong relationships and ultimately winning the battle against your competitors.

You will find that in *Opening Your Presence*, Greta's approach is remarkably similar and relatable.

Opening Your Presence

I now work in an executive role in the world's largest hospitality company with the most amount of rooms, and Greta has taught me how to present myself in a way that allows me to win with large audiences compared to my early days of checking individual guests in and out of hotel rooms.

We all deal with many different audiences every day, but too often we make the mistake of communicating with them in the same fashion.

When I first met Greta I quickly learned what it meant to adjust to your audience. I had a comfort zone that clearly needed to be expanded and I had finally found a trusted partner who could help me do that in smart, very practical ways.

After you read this book you will be well-equipped to do the same. The best presentation in the world is of no value if you do not reach the people to whom you are speaking.

Greta's methods will allow you to tailor her suggestions no matter what the industry, need or audience.

What I appreciate about Greta is that I finally met someone who could take me way beyond theory. In this book, you will discover not just the what and why, but also *how* to do it. That is how she took someone like myself, and helped me go from a deliverer of good messages to great ones. This includes not only one-on-one meetings or presentations, but also speaking on large stages in front of hundreds of people, sometimes in faraway places too!

Even with my fairly introverted personality, I actually can't wait to get on a big stage and put to work all the great things Greta has taught me.

By the way, if you ever get to meet her in person, you will find a special person who is fun, outgoing, a great listener, and incredibly genuine in her love for her clients.

In *Opening Your Presence*, you will experience her personality coming through as she offers stories from her vast experiences as a coach and a consultant. The exercises you will find throughout the book are very simple and yet the perspective they offer lays a foundation for the objectivity and perspective that can be so difficult to develop.

Within these chapters is something for anyone who has ever struggled to be heard, whether it was with an audience of one, a few or several hundred. I hope you get out of your time with Greta as much as I have and you too, come to call her a "Trusted Advisor."

Shawn McAteer
Vice President – Brand Management
Full Service Brands
Hilton Worldwide

Introduction

Open Your Presents and Open Your Presence

Your presence *is* a present… It is made up of several unique gifts, meant to be shared with your audience.

We perform every day, making mini-presentations before all kinds of audiences – our spouses, children, boss, team and club members – and when you share your individuality, your *essence*, and bring all that to the table for the world to see, you are indeed tapping into presents (talents, tastes, personality, quirks, mannerisms, voice) that make you uniquely you.

However, your ability to confidently connect with the audience, the message, or even yourself is tested by a vast array of influences, sometimes out of your control. Here, we will focus on what you do control. And it's more than you may think.

In my role as a coach and consultant, I've interacted with thousands of people seeking to present themselves in the most successful way possible. They often make one particular stipulation: "I just want to be myself (i.e. natural, me, etc.)"

Well, me too! There's no one I'd rather someone be. But, for a multitude of reasons, these same people twist themselves into pretzels to act like someone they think they are *supposed* to be and wind up detached from their most authentic self.

Their greatest gifts and assets (the components of their presence) are eclipsed by well-meaning choices.

Take that in for a moment.

Do you relate? In the heat of the moment, you can't think of what you'd like to say and, if you do, can't find the best way to say it.

When you are required to do a presentation in your office, nerves may prevent you from speaking with authority and conviction even about a project you supervised! One unnatural act deserves another, which leads to another and voilà... You are the pretzel.

If this were a yoga pose, it would feel as painful it looks. But with sheer determination and practice, even the most convoluted and possibly excruciating "pose" can be maintained and even begin to feel normal.

I've seen it with my own eyes: people who have strayed so far from what is genuine and delightfully compelling to cling to artificial façades believing it to be "natural."

The communication challenges people face and the subsequent reasoning behind their presentation choices vary and are as complex as the individuals and situations involved.

I have observed two primary obstacles that hinder one's ability to communicate expressively.

First, **Lack of Practice**. It's that simple. In the age of text messaging, tweets, email and whatever other format that has launched since writing this paragraph, people are unskilled in the art of face-to-face communication, *because they do it the least.*

I have met many young people currently entering the work force who speak in monotones and struggle with basic inter-personal communication. These are amazingly bright, gifted and well-educated individuals who cannot appreciate the full expression of their voices because it has laid dormant.

Their ability to convey well-formed thoughts and vocal variations, like inflection, are minimal and it is not for lack of talent! Even talking is a skill that is perfected with practice.

The second challenge I have observed in my work is a **Lack of Mindfulness**. As I will delve into more deeply, no one sees themselves objectively and the greater this issue, the greater the missteps.

Opening Your Presence

While we may never see ourselves the way others do, we all need to be cognizant of the part we play in communication.

Speakers *do* influence content. Speakers *can* sway the listener. Personality *does* matter and this *is* personal.

It is extremely valuable to embrace the significance and scope of one's unique persona. If you don't embrace the value you bring to the table, you limit your potential. Believing "it's just little ol' me" leads to passivity. It crushes the desire to improve and expand one's abilities. Even natural talent must be nurtured and cultivated.

I've seen clients go to extraordinary lengths to create an illusion rather than reach for what is authentic. I once advised a television talk show client to listen and give his attention to his co-host when she was speaking on the air. He replied, "Oh, for the audience' sake, I should pretend to listen?" I suggested he just try listening and see how that worked.

The platforms on which you present may vary greatly: boardroom, convention center, television or in your own living room.

For clarity sake, in *Opening Your Presence*, I have focused primarily on the more formal or legitimate forms of presentation; the kinds you might do as part of your job, a volunteer position or hobby. These might be daily, monthly or simply once in a while. The groups you address may be large, small or one-on-one; maybe you are required to use a microphone, PowerPoint® presentation software or visual aids.

But if you feel challenged by indecision or unable to say what you mean in a manner that feels genuine, I want you to know that you are not alone in the struggle for personal objectivity.

In a sea of biases, almost everyone I've ever met with has hated some aspect of themselves (voice, hair, height, freckles) and in almost every case I found the objectionable item to be either unnoticeable or one of his or her most engaging qualities.

Obsession on the trivial serves as a distraction from what is attainable. I've worked with perfectionists who scrutinize minor details, as well as individuals who operate with their eyes closed, taking wild swings at a foul ball hoping to make contact.

Many people make unrealistic comparisons and some believe the unexamined life is the only one worth living. The underlying thread weaving through us all is that we are not able to see ourselves objectively and therefore, our best efforts may be unrewarding.

Most of us have a commentator in our heads: you know, the one who whispers cruel nothings into our ear. Yours may be repeating the same message on an endless loop, and you don't know how to make it stop.

I will discuss how to turn down the volume and even change the channel to focus on what is truly important and productive.

> *I believe all human beings have a desire to be seen and heard, truly seen and heard, as the individual he or she is and that means untwisting the pretzel.*

I offer this illustrated guidebook[1] to start the process towards a more authentic and successful means of expression.

The personal stories I share may mirror your own challenges. I've encapsulated years of observations, exercises and concepts so that you may privately customize them for your presentations or "performance."

All interactions are a kind of performance and most of us judge the success or failure of these performances – in life, jobs, relationships and specific projects – irrationally or

---

[1] The bulk of these illustrations are not in the literal sense, although I hope you enjoy my illustrator's artistry. I've dug deep for enlightening (I hope), entertaining (you tell me) and, above all, true stories and examples so that you may come to a deeper appreciation of you own gifts and challenges. Names and situations have been slightly altered to respect anonymity and protect the embarrassed.

emotionally. Let's try a little less emotion and more playing fair. No bullying!

It is empowering on several levels to understand how we send and receive messages. So we're going to start with some basics. This will serve as your launch pad, but the final destination, how fast or slowly you go, and ultimately the exact route, are up to you.

I hope that what "they" see is what *you* get – heard and seen as the truly unique person you are. You are always making an impression. **What does what you say, say about you?**

The more accurate question may be: "What does *how* you speak, say about you?"

It is time to open those presents, but first, a commercial break for...

Me!

Consider the Source, Please

When I meet anyone heeding bad advice from well-meaning individuals who have no idea what they're talking about, it is usually because it was said powerfully and with tremendous conviction. I think it is wise to always consider the source. What makes this person such an authority? I strongly suggest doing your due diligence to find out what lies behind this person who just told you to pat your head and rub your tummy while tapping your foot.

In that vein, I thought it might interest you to know…

…aside from a degree in Drama and Communications, I worked in theater, film, television and radio for almost 20 years before becoming a full-time coach and consultant. Before I coached it, I did it. *A lot.*

I stood before the camera, sometimes shoulder-to-shoulder with major celebrities. I toured nationally and performed in every live venue from cabarets, theaters, shopping malls and rodeos to Off-Broadway and New York's Lincoln Center.

I served as a product spokesperson in hundreds of radio and television commercials for every product and industry from diamonds, video games, banks, lotteries, running shoes, chili, pharmaceuticals and home permanents. I took a BC® Powder and came back strong, marveled at the juiciness of Church's® fried chicken, served Miller® beer, won the lottery, and modeled clothes for JCPenney®.

I also did film and television. I was a nurse, bank teller, housewife, librarian, waitress, and hair dresser. I served time in the slammer, called Bingo, went back to prison, sold real estate, clerked in a dime store… All from the comfort of a movie set, TV studio or recording booth.

I worked with film directors like Oliver Stone and Robert Altman and stood face-to-face with great actors like Brian Dennehy, Gary Oldman, Kevin Costner, Marcia Gay Harden, Cloris Leachman and Richard Gere... even Barney, the purple dinosaur. Yet, except for the photo on the jacket of this book, we might pass each other in the Halls of Anonymity.

Because I've been there, done that, I know about nerves and insecurity, about not having prepared adequately and the down side of being *overly* prepared. I know about twisting myself into a pretzel and I know about human cruelty – how easy it is to fall into the trap of believing a stranger's horrible, mean-spirited comment instead of listening to myself.

From my involvement in hundreds of productions of all sizes, I learned the value of team work; serving the greater good of a project and not just myself. I learned that it wasn't always about me. Heck, it was rarely about me!

Even when you are the "main attraction," the power of the team is what truly defines a success.

> *I once starred in a Church's Fried Chicken commercial, where I was required to bite into a chicken leg and exclaim "how juicy!" This required take after take, which meant bite after bite. An actor can't possibly swallow every bite of food in every take.*

I will always have a soft spot in my heart for the crew member who lay at my feet holding the bucket into which I spit un-swallowed chicken. This guy was hilarious — always making me laugh and not feel self-conscious.

After an entire morning of this, with many more to go, we broke for lunch. He cheerfully offered me his arm and said, "Shall I escort you to the lunch room? I hear we're having chicken."

This man's professionalism and humor enabled me to do my job under stressful, often unflattering conditions.

Spit-Bucket Man, wherever you are, I salute you!

So how (or why) did I transition to coaching full-time?

The "how" part is easy. I answered the phone. But that phone call came at the perfect moment, following an interesting conversation with my agent.

She gave me exciting news about an audition, for which I was the prototype.

"They want a 'Greta Muller' type," she said. Wow! How flattering.

"What time is my audition?" I asked.

"Oh, they didn't ask to see *you*, just someone *like* you!"

Really? Check, please. Call me a Thanksgiving turkey and put a fork in me. I was done.

The phone call, the momentous one that changed the course of my life, was in reference to a position as a Talent Coach for Talent Dynamics, an industry leader in television broadcast coaching and placement.

"Talent" is the term used in reference to all kinds of on-air professionals and the job meant traveling to TV stations across the country, working with news, weather and sports anchors and reporters on their communication and performance skills. That was almost 17 years ago.

In *Outliers: The Story of Success*, Malcolm Gladwell expounds on the theory that 10,000 hours of experience create the foundation for expert status in one's field.

By the time I started coaching full-time, I had already accrued my 10,000+ hours as a performer. By the time I moved to New York in 2005, I had been coaching full-time for almost 7 years, as much as 120 days a year on the road, often working 8, 10 and 12-hour days... You do the math.

I understand and appreciate Mr. Gladwell's theory as I think of the confidence and skillset I have built as a result of all my years of experience. Mix in training and research and I believe I have something more than a personal opinion to offer. But there is more.

Just as I interact with people whose communication style is a reflection of layers and layers of experiences and beliefs, I too bring to the table everything that made me, me. As a child, my dream was to become a teacher. I was a victim of cruel bullying as a child. Throw in some alcoholic family dynamics that led to therapy, Al-Anon and eventually the School of Practical Philosophy on New York's Upper East Side... *All* of this, I embrace in my work. Being a coach taps into everything I love about mentoring and nurturing talents.

I hope you will see yourself more clearly and hear *your* truth through simple instructions that I believe break down complex communication dynamics.

I don't claim to reinvent the presentation wheel and goodness knows, there must be hundreds (thousands?) of books about communication. Finding the one that resonates with you is invaluable. More than a "how to," think of this as a "why to."

I want you to do some introspection and decide for yourself what makes you special. Really. I want you to be able to answer the question "Why you?"

If you want to be told what to do without having to think, this is not your guide. And if what you want is an official sounding business-eze, you might be disappointed. I'm from the South and I write much like I talk.

I want you to smile, even laugh, at yourself and know that you are not alone. Most likely, you'll read about someone who has the exact same challenge, which may be comforting.

I hope what you find here frees you from a limited comfort zone that's been inhibiting your ability to confidently step up to the podium as the communicator of your dreams.

I encourage you to listen for your voice, the one within; the one that might have gotten squashed or taken a detour. As you read, I ask that you be willing to try a new idea on for size and then fine-tune it and make your own.

Think of this as a guided tour and it is your voice on the headset. Ultimately, it is not about listening to me. It is about listening to yourself.

Chapter 1.   It's Time to Shop!

No money is required, but there are four basic concepts that are the very foundation of incredible and credible presentations. If you think of your message as a product, something you ask your audience to "buy," it's important that you buy (accept) the practicality of these ideas in order to fully embrace your power as Messenger.

I will examine each in more detail throughout the book, but here is a quick sweep of what I believe is important to buy before you check out.

Concept Number One

People buy you...
before they buy your product.

Say it with me: People buy *you* (or don't) before they buy (or not) whatever it is that you're pitching.

No matter where you are, what you're selling, or who you are selling it to, you are being judged, scrutinized and assessed *first*.

Never was this more crystal clear than when I met with a cosmetic salesperson who wore no cosmetics herself! She was an independent rep for an online company and the bulk of her sales were done through in-home demonstrations. She was struggling with low sales and asked that I observe her in action.

When I pointed out that she wore no make-up, she exclaimed, "Is that important?" I don't know about you, but I would be hesitant to buy anything from someone who did not use it personally.

Your "product" may be a thought, an idea, concept, project or, get this – it may be a tangible product like a toaster – but you are the seller. As such, you want other people (buyer = audience) to not just hear words coming out of your mouth, **but *hear* what you *mean*.**

You are the packaging by which your product (the message) is sold.

This is the most important concept for us to agree on. It's the one on which all the others are based. If you don't believe that you are a vital component in the reception, rejection and perceived value of the message, you are kidding yourself.

Regardless of the industry, venue, audience size or type, you have incredible potential that should not be over-looked, trivialized or under-used.

I've had clients push back (something which I welcome whole-heartedly) with the following arguments: "Can't I simply present the facts?" "Can't I just say what I mean?" "Won't my passion or knowledge come through naturally?"

Maybe and maybe not.

Let's say that your job requires you to present weekly updates in interdepartmental meetings. Yes, this is a presentation and may be more important than you think. Sometimes, there just doesn't seem to be much going on.

Roger, over there, makes his department sound like the very hub of activity every single week, while you struggle with the monotonous details of a long-term project. Sometimes, you "cut and paste" from last week's presentation, which works fine. It's a only status report. Who cares?

Where is all that natural passion that is supposed to infuse your delivery? How are you to sound interesting if you don't find it fundamentally compelling or important?

Let's talk about who cares when Roger's department gets the funding and yours doesn't. How about Roger's raise and promotion? The one you wanted.

Could it be that Roger's dynamic storytelling skills influenced the boss's decisions? I'll bet it seems important now.

Perhaps sounding calm and professional is your challenge. You are so emotionally invested in your product that you find yourself overwhelmed, angry or falling into a puddle of tears. Putting your thoughts together in any sort of organized manner is a struggle.

Can't you just say what you mean?

I don't know. Can you?

As the seller of a message, you want to mimic the merchant who cultivates satisfied customers. The merchant keeps his customers happy by creating an environment, product and message centered on one basic premise: *You are important to me.*

A successful presenter has the same objectives.

"People buy *you* before they buy your product" is a simple way of saying that **people determine credibility of the speaker first**.

How much value you possess as a trusted resource depends on how you answer the question, "Why should an audience listen to me?" and more importantly, "Why should they *believe* me?"

People may associate a higher value with the product (message) based on your perceived value as the seller. Notice I said *"perceived"* value. That is because in the communication world, perception is everything. **Perception of the truth *is* the truth.**

Have you noticed the high number of infomercials that use pitch people (sellers) with foreign accents? This is an intentional choice dictated by research and company cultures.

Typically, the accents used in these kinds of commercials are British and, more recently, Australian.[2] Pronunciation and enunciation are crisp and clean so words are easily understood and there can be no association to any particular area of the United States. Immediately, someone with this foreign, exotic accent is thought to be more credible and the dialect is an immediate attention-getter.

Numerous factors contribute to the acceptability of the speaker. Don't get me started on the perceived physical perfection of television anchors, hosts or pitch people. (I said "perceived.")

While this is not true 100% of the time (there's Larry King, who started on radio by the way), extensive testing and manipulation are often performed to achieve the particular

---

[2] Other accents may sound sexy or exotic, but are not quite so melodic to an American ear.

look and presentation style that increases viewer trust and reception.

Are you getting the idea that there is more to this communication game than meets the eye? Or perhaps, what meets the eye is most important? We'll talk more about that soon.

Concept Number Two

Many people do not hear what you mean,
they hear what they think…

This is why it is extremely important to be crystal clear about your intention and manner, because what they "hear" is highly influenced by personal points of reference.

As the drawing illustrates, someone waiting to hear about their own promotion will not be excited by your news of such, even if they are being given a new assignment.

The man who's off to play golf only heard what he wanted to hear – the boss is away, so on Friday I play!

Even a child knows not to ask Mom for a treat when she is angry. She's more likely to say "no."

The same theory applies in professional communications. However, you may not have the benefit of determining the right time and place to make your presentation. This does not mean you stop communicating.

Other culprits blur the lines of communication, as well.

- **Shrinking attention span.** As digital options grow, the average attention span shrinks. Anyone who is texting, listening to music, reading or otherwise engaged while you are speaking cannot possibly appreciate nuance and innuendo.[3]
- **Likeability.** Think of one of your personal trusted advisors, someone you truly respect and regard as trustworthy. I predict this is someone you think

---

[3] Here is an excellent article on multi-tasking and its effect on message comprehension, posted on the Colorado State University's website called "Students Think They Can Multitask. Here's Proof They Can't." bit.ly/studentscantmultitask

highly of and, yes, like. How many people do you dislike *and* trust? Likeability and acceptance go hand in hand.

- **The Master Translator.** This person rarely takes any message at face value. They do not easily trust and therefore they spend more energy trying to figure out what the speaker is *really* trying to say and less time on the message itself.

Concept Number Two may seem insurmountable, but embracing any challenge provides a platform for options. We will go into these options soon.

Concept Number Three

"What feels right, must be right...Right?" NOT!

Anything, and I mean *anything*, can feel normal and comfortable, if done enough. Just ask that woman in the 6" heels who swears she can't leave home without them. You may be taking all kinds of distracting tics and habits onto the stage or into the conference room simply because they *feel* normal.

I've seen speakers pick their teeth, nose and clothing, click their nails, blink furiously, never blink, cry, snort, squeak and more, never realizing for a second how distracting, confusing and annoying that particular habit may be *to the audience!*

It felt good to them or, worse, it felt like nothing at all, so they didn't realize they were doing it. And those are just the unconscious moves.

I've seen, and you probably have as well, speakers who make conscious choices they believe are effective. It feels like the right thing to do, but from the vantage point of the audience member, it is not. Examples are screaming, reading note cards verbatim, pacing back and forth, gripping both sides of a podium, etc.

There is always a period of adjustment as you un-learn some old tricks and try new ones. That means a certain amount of discomfort.

I cannot promise you, nor should anyone else, that overcoming performance anxiety is easy or comfortable. That idea is right up there with the one pill to make you magically lose all your excess weight without exercise or diet!

Hmm... Maximizing your presence into great presentations doesn't work that way and the magic weight loss pill doesn't exist. If it did, we'd all be on television and we'd all be skinny.

But I can promise you this. Spend enough time outside of your comfort zone and even new skills can and will begin to feel... Yes, comfortable!

If we are truly successful, you will find that a period of adjustment brings you closer to what is more natural and genuine in the first place.

I have often worked with people who had suppressed their natural impulses in a misguided decision to mimic someone else. In our work, they discover that the very impulse they had avoided is the very thing they return to. They opened their presence.

This brings me to our 4th buy-in, and probably one of the most important to embrace.

Concept Number Four

No one, and I mean no one,
sees himself or herself objectively.

It is fundamentally impossible. You also cannot see yourself as others see you and guess what? How others see you varies greatly! Acckkkk! So what's a person to do?

All is not lost. I said you didn't see yourself objectively. However, you can *gain objectivity* and it is important that you do. This goes a long way in making better choices, possibly more natural and genuine choices, which get you seen and heard.

Before we move on, here's a quick recap:

1. People buy you before they buy what you're selling.
2. People may not "hear" what you say; but hear what they *think* you said based on their position, mood or desire.
3. If it feels good, it's probably an old habit and it's time to try something new!
4. People do not see themselves objectively.

Throughout this book, I will refer to these concepts, exploring the depth and breadth of their validity and your options. Let's begin with a closer examination though of 3 and 4.

Chapter 2.   Doin' What Comes Naturally and the Road to Perdition

I mentioned the most common request I hear from clients in the introduction: "I just want to be myself!"

This is typically followed closely by the most frequently asked question: "Can't I just do what feels natural?"

In my experience, this translates to: "I don't *want* to do anything uncomfortable/different. I just want you to confirm that what I'm doing (who I am) is already good enough."

I have learned that I am unable to *make* someone believe he or she is anything. Instead, I work to provide the means for their own realizations.

Recognizing that one is "good enough" is at the crux of wanting to be seen and heard. As human beings we have a desire for our existence to be validated. We seek this validation daily, whether we realize it or not and when we *do* realize it, no one wants to consult a coach to find out that who they are isn't good enough.

Opening Your Presence

So let me say right off the bat: You *are* "good enough." You're probably terrific and I don't even know you. But I have yet to meet one person who didn't bring something unique, special and valid to the presentation arena. The most common enemy to having a realistic self-awareness (notice I don't say "positive" or "idealistic") is being too focused on the one thing he or she *doesn't* have or *can't* do.

When faced with public speaking, most people have a concept of what they believe a great public speaker is: powerful, booming voice; naturally confident and out-going; never gets nervous; great looking, smooth, at ease in front of crowds, etc.

"And then there's little ol' me. I'm none of those things." I've heard variations of this expressed a thousand times.

A few tidbits:

- Billy Graham, powerful evangelist and speaker, confessed to being a shy child.
- James Earl Jones ("Darth Vader") was once a stutterer.
- John Malkovich, John Lennon and Angelina Jolie have all admitted to hating the sound of their own voice.

Giving in to what is natural is not the same as embracing one's talents and strengths and choosing a path for achieving the best possible outcome.

And while we're on the subject of "natural," there is nothing natural about speaking to a group of people, especially strangers. The larger the crowd, the more formal the presentation and the more unnatural it is... *unless you do it often*. Most of the people I work with are not professional speakers. They serve in other capacities and are called upon to present a particular message from time to time. Big difference.

While we are on the subject of natural and easy, it stands to reason that what we do most often increases in strength and becomes more polished. In this day and age of cell phones, texting, emails and all things digital, it only makes sense that speaking in front of an audience may induce anxiety *simply because we do it the least*.

I'm sure you don't relish the thought of risking embarrassment or humiliation. So how can you be sure something is right, if it doesn't *feel* right?

Great question!

And to answer that question we must spend a few minutes exploring...

Imagine if you will... A world in which, if it *feels* right, it must be good.

Ah, if only that were true!

> *While visiting a television station, I personally witnessed a sports anchor dig in his ear (yes, on live television) with his pencil during cross-talk (that sometimes inane chit-chat between stories) with the two main anchors. Perhaps out of boredom, an unconscious desire to communicate his feelings, or maybe he had an itch, but this anchor dug in his ear with the pointed end of his pencil, took it out and then proceeded to look at what was on the tip. On the air!*

How did this happen? It was natural. It was comfortable. This was an extremely experienced anchor. Sitting in front of that camera was as familiar to him as the operating room is to the skilled surgeon: intimidating and confusing to me, but completely natural to the surgeon.

Without staying focused on the ultimate, positive outcome, we all run the risk of being too comfortable and *there is such a thing as being too comfortable*!

Let's look at some other factors that mislead speakers who try to use "comfort" as a barometer for presentation success.

My Audience is Who?

Would you rather see friendly, familiar faces in the audience or a roomful of strangers? A few or many? Small space or large auditorium?

Whatever your responses, there is someone who feels the complete opposite.

You may be comforted knowing that your mother will be smiling from the front row or that detail may fill you with dread. Whoever sits in your audience, the awareness of their presence leads to a skewed sensibility and inhibits one's ability to be objective.

Why?

Because in the world of presentations the Comfort Zone is a little like the Twilight Zone:

> *What something feels like (especially when standing in front of 20 – 200 people) is not how it is perceived.*

This is why Concept Number Three is so relevant.

When that spotlight is on and you are feeling pressure to perform, nothing feels "normal" or has proper perspective.

The pause you took while searching for the exact word felt like an hour. In reality, it was 1.5 seconds.

That stumble as you approached the podium felt like a slow-motion train wreck with body parts (yours) being strewn across the screen in high definition. Really, no one noticed.

Perhaps you came off that same podium feeling like you knocked it out of the park. Your swagger and smile reflect the confidence of someone who just hit a home run. Whoo-hoo!

Why? I don't know... Because that toilet tissue dragging off your heel and the spinach in your teeth were hilarious. The whole section you forgot to mention left everyone scratching their heads and don't get me started on your 79 PowerPoint slides, but Hallelujah! You got through it without throwing up. That alone is enough for you to breathe a sigh of relief.

How we define or measure success is in direct proportion to how quickly we improve and ultimately gain confidence and... You guessed it, *comfort*!

Yes, eventually you will have comfort, I promise you. Just don't look for it too soon.

Unless you are a robot or king of the world, you most likely have feelings about giving a presentation. Emotions vary greatly and depend on variables such as one's personality type, subject matter, rehearsal, preparation, advanced warning, urgency, outcome import or possibly how much caffeine is in your system.

Below is a finely tuned, highly professional (not!) scale for measuring your level of comfort prior to the start of a presentation.

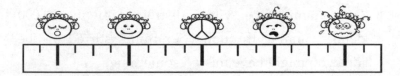

Whether you are so Zen that you are almost asleep or you are sweating bullets, where (and how) you end has a great deal to do with where you begin. You may never love giving presentations, buy my goal is to help you get centered and make peace with the idea.

While I am not a psychologist by any stretch, through the years I have certainly observed emotional reactions and been placed in a position to deal with them. As I mentioned I have witnessed consistencies in the way people respond to their challenges, which often coincides with personality types.

Here are a few of the people I've met. Perhaps you can relate to one.

- **The Perfectionist** – The "Nothing is worth doing if it isn't done perfectly" type. You feel preparation is directly proportional to success so you finesse and tweak every word and detail, fine-tuning your presentation until it is letter and picture-perfect.

  You might approach the podium with extreme confidence knowing that no stone was left un-turned. *Or* you might be wildly distracted by the 10,000 details running through your mind, stirred by the idea you might have missed something.

  You do not have the brain space to notice that half of your audience is looking at their cell phones checking important Solitaire moves, uh, I mean messages. The other half is yawning. Every single detail is important and *you* thought of everything! Or did you?

  As you leave the podium you think of another little nugget you should have included, another slide to make that point, a better word, a prettier scarf, better suit, more laminated hand-outs... Now you hate everything, especially if things didn't quite go as planned.

Since most presentations are affected by outside, uncontrollable variables, very few are perfect and therefore that quest for perfection is the perfect excuse for imperfection. It's a vicious cycle.

- **The Control Freak** – A sister companion to the Perfectionist, you are the "nothing is worth doing if you don't do it yourself" type. Your plate overflows with projects that must receive 110% of your time and energy, and only yours. No one can be trusted to do the kind of job you do.

Projects large or small, significant or trivial all get your undivided attention and prioritizing. What's that? Too bad you don't have anything left for your family, health and enjoyment. You have no way to gauge presentation success or failure. Everything could be better, if only you had a little more time.

- **The Fly-by-the-Seat-of-the-Pants Speaker** – There's no such thing as perfect, so let's settle for pretty good. Well, adequate is fine. Yes, you like to wing it and improvise. You often throw things together at the last minute and you haven't gotten fired yet.

You're a pretty funny guy and chances are charm and humor can deflect attention from content.

As long as you don't go blank or throw up, it's acceptable. You are familiar with the material, so you scratch a few notes or create some bullet points. You might make a last minute mental note. "Oh, yeah! Don't forget to mention so and so."

But you do forget and stammer searching for that right word...

Luckily, you're a pretty funny guy and can make people laugh. So what if your credibility is questionable? They won't make the mistake of asking you to do this again!

But once again, the promotion goes to that jerk in the suit. Yes, you forgot your tie, but how important is that?

- **Color Me Blue... or Red, or Maybe Orange?** – Your performance depends on your mood. You work by *feel*! And today is not a good one. Perhaps you overcompensate for the lack of preparation by talking loudly and making jokes at your own expense. In a caffeine blur, you cram, just like college days.

You might over-explain. You might say little. It all depends. You may try to disappear and curl into a roly-poly bug. *The smaller I am, the less they can see!*

The speaker before you had some top-notch slides and a handout. Why didn't you think of that?

Afterward, you kick yourself all the way to a friendly ear or nearest bar hoping someone can help you feel better. People tell you it was fine and so you convince yourself they are right. You don't do this often, so why worry about it and… You're off! There you go running to another appointment you weren't in the mood for.

You may identify strongly with one of these types or you may see bits of yourself in all of the above. Now comes the question...

What's a Person to Do?

When it comes to presentations, many people don't know what works, how to prepare, how to best address their colleagues, how to stand, use their hands, where to look…

Even when you are willing and able, you might be happy to blend into the background or just let Ralph do it. Only Ralph is out sick. Uh-oh. You *have* to do it!

Opening Your Presence

You fly into action, doing what you usually do, not even thinking about its effectiveness, but at least it's familiar. It's fine. Everyone knows you're not a professional speaker and they aren't that much better. You're sure they'll understand.

You keep thinking you'll get better at this, maybe get some coaching, practice, read a book, or do *something*, but it's not a big deal until it is a big deal. And then, it's too late.

The moment of truth has arrived and now it's time to get up in front of an audience.

Let's see if any of these thoughts have run through your head as you face the faces staring back:

- You hate that you are so nervous, which makes you more nervous.
- You flip through your note cards and now you hate your opening, your graphics, your dog and you don't want to budge. Your feet feel like cement. You can't believe you wore this suit, your hair is out of control and there's that guy... You notice the one guy in the room who isn't listening. You can't take your eyes off of him. Inwardly you are screaming, "Look at me! You are supposed to be listening to *me!*" You must gain the attention of this one person or the speech is a failure.

- Nothing sounds the way it did in your head. You are not moving or acting quite as dynamically as you had hoped. Why can't you act natural?
- You feel a trickle of sweat. You are convinced it is the size of a bolder and everyone can see it running down your cheek.
- Your voice broke and you sound like a little girl. You are no longer a competent, intelligent researcher. You are a 12-year-old with braces. Why did you eat spinach at lunch? What were you thinking?

I'll tell you what you're *not* thinking. You are not thinking about your message and how to sell it. You haven't any brain space left for audience benefit, message reception or message retention.

It is impossible to concentrate on the message when your brain is in the Mental Olympics.

Opening Your Presence starts when you replace unrealistic distractions with reasonable goals.

And the first step is acceptance of what is. Make a list, check it, and look at it as unemotionally as possible. This is not a time for judgments.

Let's take nerves as an example. You have a presentation and you feel nervous. Admit it. This is the way it is. It is

25

perfectly natural. Lots of people get nervous. You don't have to like it, just embrace it as true.

I once told a client how natural it is to feel nervous and he pushed back with, "Well, how about you? I'll bet you never get nervous." Hah! Now that's funny. Of course I do.

I've had the fortune of being nervous and having to perform under pressure so many times that this emotional pressure became my friend. I use the extra adrenaline to my advantage. And I learned a little secret about nerves.

Nervousness is not what screws us up.

It is our physical and emotional responses to those nerves that create problems.

Beating yourself up for being nervous is more destructive than being nervous.

We are called on to make assessments and judgments thousands of times a day. You get a tingle in the back of your neck alerting you to danger and you respond. These are the very instincts that keep us safe in certain situations.

Many typical responses to performance anxiety are unproductive and only heighten the apprehension: shallow breathing, clenched teeth, stiff body language, mental obsessing... These all intensify and prolong the negative experience.

You have many options, which you may personalize, that actually help the nervous energy work to your advantage.

When you embrace your apprehension as normal and incorporate deep breathing and physical movements to release nervous energy, you are more likely to warm up before a presentation.

But you can't take these steps if you're too busy beating yourself up for being nervous in the first place!

In the presentation world, solutions follow close behind recognition without judgment. You aren't weird and different. Even Susie Cool over there, who may not *appear* nervous, has some anxiety.

Perception is everything. As long as Susie doesn't let on that she is scared stiff, how do you know what's going on in her head?

The same is true for you. Projecting an outward sense of calm (fake it till you make it) while your stomach is rolling is the next best thing to *being* calm. And guess what? An action done consistently can foster the corresponding feeling. You *are* calmer. I've seen it happen many times.

"I Don't Work by Feel.
I Listen to What People Tell Me"

This may sound familiar. I have clients tell me all the time that they ask for honest criticism and are open to constructive feedback.

So you think that others are going to tell you the truth and this will be helpful?

When it comes to feedback, *who* you listen to, *how much* you listen and even *when* you listen is a tricky proposition.

"My mother is a straight shooter. She is always raving to her friends about how wonderful I am."

Your mother thinks you're terrific? Shocking.

"But, I ask for *honest* feedback. I tell my wife I want to know what she *really* thinks."

Oh, really?

Rarely are loved ones able to offer truly helpful, constructive feedback. Love may be blind or love may intensify the view.

Yes, loved ones may heap on well-meaning accolades and bathe you in a comforting coat of praise. There are also those for whom familiarity breeds scrutiny. They believe it in your best interest to harp on trivialities that stand in the way of perfection.

Family members are primarily driven by emotion and familiarity. Your audience most likely doesn't know you as well as your wife, thank goodness.

What about colleagues? These are professionals after all. Certainly *they* can offer productive input.

Choose what colleagues to trust carefully. There may be jealousy, spite or perhaps idolization at play. Even a well-meaning, relatively neutral co-worker may not know how to offer advice or may just have bad taste!

> A female anchor client dramatically changed her reading style between one of my station consultation visits to the next. In a few months, she had dropped her voice to a hoarse whisper and had lost her warm, conversational style.
>
> When I asked her what had happened, she told me she had been trying new things and "John told me he really liked it."
>
> "Who is John?" I asked, thinking it was a new boyfriend.
>
> "You know... The camera operator."
>
> "That John? The 19-year-old college freshman?"

John was a nice kid who worked part-time to help pay for school.

Whether John wanted to be liked, felt overwhelmed by this hometown icon, or was expressing a genuine feeling, I was more surprised by the lengths to which this anchor adjusted to his adolescent input.

When I mentioned this she said it never occurred to her to not listen. This was a perfect example of not considering the source.

You most likely do not seek input from those you do not like or trust, but how often have you pursued constructive feedback from a busy supervisor who simply does not possess the time, skill or verbiage to express it adequately?

Everyone is biased. Everyone has personal tastes and agendas affected by *their* experiences. Finding objective, truly helpful critiques from close friends, family and colleagues is rare.

Add to the equation, your biases, phobias, fears, goals and perceptions, and the communication conduit is incredibly small.

This is why learning to trust yourself – on a more objective and ultimately healthy level – gives you the proper filter through which all this input flows.

Finally, We All Dig in Our Ears...
Because It Just Feels So Darn Good

Just like the ear-digging sportscaster I mentioned, it might feel good to dig in our ears, but it won't win anyone an Emmy.

By definition, a rut is familiar and familiarity breeds insensitivity. You lose touch with the goal because you've been down that road a million times. In fact, let's look at the road on which you go to and from work. You've done it five days a week for six years. Maybe you've done the research and you are absolutely convinced you know the shortest, most efficient path home while avoiding tolls and too many lights.

This is not the only way home, but anyone with sense would know it's the best way home, right? And the first time you offer your neighbor a ride, he asks you why you go *this* way like you were a Neanderthal. And what's worse? When you hear his route, it *is* shorter! Ugh!

Come Monday morning, what route do you take? Yours. Why? Because you like it. It feels normal. It feels like the right way. You're going to need a lot more than Mr. Know-It-All to get you to take a different route.

Everyone has an opinion and almost everyone believes theirs is the right one. And it may be, for them!

Heeding advice from the mailman, your mother, boss, priest, handyman and coffee barista is just as dangerous as listening to no one. At some point you must set out to determine what is working and what isn't. And that may take you outside of that comfort zone.

Opening Your Presence

You mean you want me to experience discomfort? Yes.

Risk humiliation? Possibly.

The most comforting thought right now may be to put down this book. But I hope you won't. Not before we do a little spring cleaning.

Chapter 3. Spring Cleaning

To fully appreciate Concept Number Four, "No one sees themselves objectively," we are going to do something similar to the spring cleaning of my youth. This yearly ritual meant *major* cleaning, shifting, lifting and purging.

"Out with the old," we were told, "to make way for the new," and this was only possible with the light that shone through streak-free windows.

You have two chores to tackle in order to identify what is "old" – impractical, inefficient, downright erroneous or phony – to make room for the "new."

Let's clean those **smudged mirrors** and **dirty filters**.

Got Windex?

Just how do you see yourself? And who is the *real* you?

Just like this man peering into the mirror, we rarely see a truly accurate reflection.

This applies on a physical level, as when we look into a mirror, as well as to internal qualities and traits.

For all you Popeyes out there declaring, "I am what I am" and that's the end of the story, I propose the idea that there is no *one* "real" anyone.

While the essence of our being remains consistent, everyone has multi-layered and multi-faceted personalities, tastes, opinions and objectives. Throw into the mix environment, social etiquette, circumstances and protocols and we are <u>all</u> a veritable cesspool of identities.

Think of **product** versus **brand**. The product is coffee, but one particular brand may evoke a more positive feeling or loyalty based on the personal preference.

You appreciate the level of quality while offering numerous choices from decaffeinated or regular, bold or mild. Depending on your taste or need you may want flavored, foam, milk, sweetened, cold, hot…

> *You are a brand and what you offer and
> how you present it, is up to you.*

The more you understand your audience and the ways your brand may entice that audience, the more options you have. I believe that to fully understand this we start with how we "see" and feel about ourselves, and that requires a closer look.

Are you the type who never looks in the mirror, afraid of what you might see? You look only when absolutely necessary. You rely on pure instinct and feeling, believing nothing that feels so right could possibly be wrong.

Opening Your Presence

Maybe you are someone who owns the 10x magnification glass to daily examine every pore, blemish and hair. Nothing gets by you! You believe in daily scrutinization, searching for flaws hoping to hide or remedy them before anyone else has a chance to notice what seems as obvious as... Just fill in the blank.

Or perhaps you live in a Carnival Fun House of Mirrors. Insecurities and moods lead to distorted, twisted and anything but fun images creating confusion and doubt. Not knowing where to go or what to do... Bam! You run into another mirror.

I believe it's important to clean the mirror as much as possible, because:

How we present ourselves is in direct relationship to how we see ourselves.

Your mirror might have some minor smudging or you may need a sand blaster to get through the layers of grunge, but standing in front of an audience distorts *any* mirror, so a certain amount of reflection on your reflection is necessary.

> **Exercise**
>
> How well do you know your face?
>
> A police sketch artist must draw an accurate resemblance based only on a witness' description, whose observation may have been mere moments.
>
> I'd like you to describe you to the sketch artist. Be as detailed as you can. Write a nice paragraph or two. You might want to keep a notebook. We'll be doing a few exercises from time-to-time. I'll be waiting for you when you are done.

How did you do? If you took this exercise seriously, many of you looked in a mirror for help, and you've had that face all of your life. Well, most of you have…

Were you able to do the exercise without attaching emotionally based, typically negative, details to your features?

I've had clients write down everything from "Jumbo's elephant ears" to "Charlie Brown face," which is not the same as saying protruding ears or a round face.

You most likely have some physical trait you wish you could change. You hate your ears while your audience may not even notice them. Perhaps they find them endearing. Clark Gable did well with them.

But your feelings about such are a distraction, which does not serve you well.

How did that mirror get so smudged? One culprit is a dirty filter. So let's see what kind of dirt is clogging the vent.

When Was the Last Time You Cleaned that Filter?

Years ago I ended a long trip with a visit to some newly married friends down in Florida. Being the wonderful houseguest I am, upon my arrival I immediately laid down for a nap.

I was out for almost two hours and when I awoke I found that my hostess decided to surprise me by doing the dirty laundry I had accumulated on my travels. Talk about room service!

She apologized for how long the dryer cycle was taking and said she thought they had bought a lemon because this new dryer was taking longer and longer to get the clothes dry! I asked when she had last cleaned the filter.

"Oh, this machine doesn't have a filter." Uh-oh. I'm sure my face revealed what I was thinking.

"I've looked! I swear. There is no filter!"

"How long have you had it?" I asked calmly.

"Almost a year."

Eek! I marched my little self into the laundry room. I was going to show her how to clean a filter! Well, I couldn't find it either. I was not about to be upstaged by a dryer, so I got on my hands and knees and took every item out of the dryer barrel and looked inside. Aha! There it was... Way in the back. Hard to see unless you knew where to look.

We both had to tug and tug and you do not want to know what came flying out of that filter. Insto-presto, my clothes were dry in a matter of minutes. Mystery solved.

The moral to the story is that humans are like dryers. We *all* have filters. They may be hard to find and without regular maintenance they become clogged. The "lint" consists of the debris from hurt feelings, education, upbringing, culture, misconceptions and, my favorite, well-meaning advice.

We must sort through hundreds of pieces of unsolicited and solicited advice, input, critiques and insults.

How you present yourself is directly affected by the junk that passes through your filter and what you do with it.

Like any household appliance, your filter needs regular maintenance. It's a dirty job but someone has to do it!

Bless Her Heart

I grew up hearing "Bless her heart" followed by some of the most tactless, often hilarious criticisms of whomever "she" was.

Probably the funniest one I ever heard went something like, "Bless her heart, she thinks she can put perfume on stink and everything's fine. Well, I've got news for her!"

Of course, she never heard this news. It was easier to go around saying "bless her heart" than to tell her she needed a good scrubbing.

Believe me, with friends and family like that, you don't need enemies. On the other hand, caustic remarks from an enemy might be easier to dismiss.

All too often, people (friends, family and colleagues) can't wait to tell you exactly what they think, some of which might actually be true. Said harshly and the filter can be damaged.

Other opinions may *not* be true, but said with conviction, they become irritants clogging that filter. Heard often enough, criticisms are absorbed into every fiber, creating a saturated filter that is useless.

Outside comments can become so ingrained you eventually forget how and where these ideas originated.

My own mother (bless her heart) was obsessed with an extreme standard of beauty, centered on the belief that you could never be thin enough. This, she imposed on her daughters. By kindergarten, I already knew which foods were dietetic and "good" and which were "bad" and made you ugly.

We received mixed signals about cleaning our plates. On one hand, there were starving children in Africa, so the food was not to be wasted. On the other, we were admonished if we did indeed clean them, and heaven help us all if we asked for seconds.

We were hounded about weight and calories until she had literally created the very food issues she hoped we would avoid. From high school to my early 20s, I swung on a food pendulum back and forth between anorexia and bulimia.

The origin of this food message blurred with time and for years I believed food to be "good" or "bad," gifted with almost supernatural powers.

I am fortunate in that I escaped the prison of bulimia or anorexia and have only small scars that now help me stay sane.

I hope your own familial influences are not so drastic. Messages from seemingly goodhearted family members can be well-intentioned, but ultimately destructive when it squashes creativity, natural development and personal respect.

We all have an inner voice. Some are louder than others. Some are downright mean. Many spew regurgitated missives making you an accidental plagiarist. If you are nagged by a harsh critic, most likely that voice is not yours.

The easiest and most unscientific way to explore this theory is to observe the way you speak to yourself. Stand back and listen to the tone and verbiage. Then ask yourself "Is this how I would speak to my child? My spouse?" Then why do you speak to yourself this way?

I worked with a gentleman who, during practice, often whispered to himself. I finally realized he was saying, "Stupid, stupid, stupid."

I was so surprised to hear this coming from a man who was the very definition of a gentleman: gracious and affable. I asked him if he said this sort of thing to his staff. He was horrified. "Of course not!"

Then why would he say it to himself? He laughed and said he hadn't put the pieces together before, but it was something his own father used to do.

I was curious. "Your father said that to you?"

He responded, "No, it was something he said to himself. My old man was terrific; very loving to his sons, but hard on himself."

This was a wonderful opportunity for us to discuss the manner in which his inner voice operated. I helped him understand that these kinds of admonishment are not helpful.

Just as children or employees are not encouraged to succeed by calling them stupid, it doesn't exactly spur you on to greatness either.

You generate that inner voice and you have the power to rewrite the script.

Acknowledge how you are spoken to by others, too. Even seemingly helpful suggestions may be misguided or, worse, intentionally cruel. I often tell clients to take nothing personally. Let me say that again.

Take. Nothing. Personally.

Consider the source and accept that unsolicited advice, especially when harsh, is rarely helpful, nor is it necessarily about you.

And if you think friends and family do a number on your self-esteem...

Ladies and Gentlemen... The Media!

On top of everything else, you are bombarded relentlessly by impeccably groomed, near perfect beautiful people in a variety of roles (talk-show hosts, spokespeople, models, actors) in a multitude of venues: billboards, magazines, television, film, product packaging, reality programming, infomercials, the internet and more.

Is it any wonder when we feel we don't measure up?

Comparisons with television stars and models are ridiculous (although many of us do it), when you consider the amount of lighting, spritzing, airbrushing and computer manipulation that goes on.[4] Did you know that due to the

---

[4] For a powerful example of why you should never compare yourself with magazines or television, here is an amazing video showing the magic of Photoshop. bit.ly/photoshopmagic

introduction of HDTV even small market, local news anchors often apply their make-up foundation with an airbrush? These are women *and* men.

The model you now envy may have been traumatized by her growth spurt at age 12, which sent her towering above every boy her age. I hope she is now laughing all the way to the bank and embracing every glorious inch she once hated.

Remember, no one evaluates you by the same standards you do. They rarely notice the same "flaws" and even if they do, they may not come to the same conclusions. Assessments, good or bad, are personal to the observer.

As an example, let's take your voice. What you hear is quite different from anyone else. What you think or feel about it is most assuredly skewed.

Let's exercise!

(And you don't have to go to the gym!)

You've taken a stab at a physical description. Now, imagine a stranger having to pick your voice out of a vocal line-up.

In regards to voice many people are downright oblivious or dislike it immensely, although they are quite willing to admit that it "doesn't sound like it sounds in my head." Most people complain of sounding more nasally than they thought.

In the presentation arena, familiarity breeds power, so get out your pen.

Describing your voice may be like me describing a wine. I may know what I like when I taste it, but I simply don't have the expertise or vocabulary to do it justice.

You may not know where to begin so let me help you. Start with volume. Are you a low-talker? Do people have to lean in to hear you? Perhaps you are loud.

Now move on to the quality and texture of your voice. Being the nice person I am, I've offered some adjectives below to help you.

Aim for at least five, more if you can. It might be helpful to use the recording device on your cell phone while you read a paragraph of something that interests you. You can also tell a personal story or recount an event at work.

Listen to the playback as though you were listening to a stranger. Then, choose the words that best describe what you hear.

airy	shrill	authoritative
soft	cheerful	tentative
light	nasal	surprised
diminutive	animated	alert
passive	tiny	dry
raspy	angry	lyrical
coarse	dynamic	credible
bold	monotone	amused
loud	passive	nervous
piercing	convincing	deep
booming	persuasive	throaty

Even professional vocalists rely on recorded playback, monitors and ear phones because no one hears themselves accurately. It's impossible.

Isn't it nice to know you are in such good company?

In order to more fully utilize this powerful instrument, it is important to release negative judgment. Some of the highest paid, most successful voice-over artists in the industry have unusual voices that are not necessarily melodious or pretty.[5] But these professionals are experienced in the art of vocal nuance and mimicry, which allows for full creative realization. They embrace the very qualities that may make another person wince.

To return to my earlier wine analogy, a sommelier may have a favorite wine, but his expertise allows him to release emotional connection in order to make highly qualified recommendations.

You may never have that kind of vocal training, nor is it necessary, but releasing emotional judgment removes extraneous obstacles.

---

[5] The first person who pops to my mind is Julie Kavner, who voices Marge Simpson on "The Simpsons." Personally I've worked with all kinds of industry professionals whose voices can be described as raspy, nasal or gravelly, yet are very successful.

Your filter didn't get clogged in one day and cannot be undone in one either. To fully realize your communication and presentation potential, you need to exercise certain muscles that may be weak from lack of use. You need practice.

Luckily, observation and assessing yourself and others is free, so practice often.

Your Window to the World

...needs a swipe and for a very good reason:

Miscommunication is not always speaker-centric
(his or her "fault"), but due in part to the listener's biases or
emotions, both conscious and unconscious.

We've all had that experience of meeting someone to whom we have an immediate dislike or negative reaction. Our senses go on alert. We may listen more intently or we may immediately disregard what this person is saying. The manner in which we receive information is damaged.

Hundreds of signals are relayed on a subconscious level to influence our discernment of message and messenger. They affect our ability to hear. An internal bias or even a headache may lead to a misunderstanding.

"I need that report," sounds like an angry accusation if you feel guilty about procrastinating. Makes sense, doesn't it?

Let's look at other ways our biases affect our ability to send as well as receive information.

People often over-compensate
for what they do not like in others.

I have observed an interesting pattern in which a client's negative feelings about a particular issue is often proportional to his or her avoidance of the same... Even when this person may not come close to having that particular challenge!

Laura

Laura, an experienced newscaster, was auditioning for a talk show host position. I was a bit surprised by her interest in the job. In the years we had worked together, I had rarely seen her demeanor vary from the somber professional viewers saw during a newscast.

As far as I was aware she did not naturally possess qualities one would normally associate with a daytime talk show host.

She asked for my help to prepare for the audition and I was thrilled. Great! This would be an ideal time to address some of these matters.

Laura began our first session emphatically declaring how much she hated "phonies," people who were overly complimentary or effusive and asked me to make sure she didn't come across as silly or "fake." Hmmm... we weren't exactly on the same page.

I had her do a relaxation exercise. We also watched tapes and practiced interview skills. I encouraged her to engage her guests, just as she would guests in her home.

Laura remained stoic in rehearsal and the audition, where she did not make it past round one. She covered her disappointment well, but I knew she was upset.

A few months later, during a subsequent visit to her station, I asked Laura if she would be willing to look at her audition tape with me. Now that time had passed and emotions had calmed, I hoped she would be able to observe herself with greater objectivity. I muted the sound so we could focus on facial expressions and body language.

After a minute or two, she stopped the tape and admitted that at the time, she thought she was performing at the level we had discussed, but now she could see how reserved and stilted she was.

We discussed her strong desire to be taken seriously. A supervisor, early in her career, had been quite harsh, often teasing her in front of co-workers. I could see this pain was still with her, motivating her serious demeanor. She was still compensating for the inexperienced novice of her youth.

In future sessions, we worked to push Laura from her comfort zone in varying degrees. We used a communication scale of 1 to 10, with 5 being a conversational level of animation for a particular story; 1 was monotone or too reserved and 10 was extreme. This scale provided the basis for comparing how something felt in performance and how it played for an audience.

This enabled Laura to gradually become a more engaging and natural storyteller, able to tap into different moods and personal levels.

Mitch

Mitch had retained my services after recently losing out on a promotion. While he was well-liked and respected he was told that he often seemed indecisive and was not seen as a leader.

It took me awhile to realize that Mitch's professional challenges were tied with his desire to be polite. He went to extremes to avoid conversational overlaps and interruptions.

I noticed Mitch hesitating in an important presentation to his colleagues. The slightest cough or comment made him pause and he seemed to have difficulty re-focusing. While colleagues jumped into lively conversations with comments or a question, Mitch raised his hand and waited for "permission" to speak.

Mitch had been raised in a strict southern home where manners and gentility were firmly enforced. Interruptions and similar "rude" behaviors were not tolerated due to his father's position in the community.

Identifying this familial influence was key to adjusting his behavior. Simply being aware helped him naturally relax and adjust to the social norm of the office.

An immediate modification was to ask his audience to hold questions. He allowed time for discussions and then stopped frequently demonstrating his authority. This resulted in fewer interruptions.

He gradually embraced the social norms of his industry, office personalities and even area of the country. In time, he came to enjoy lively group dynamics and participate more freely.

In both cases (and many others) resolution begins by recognizing the source of the issue, accepting it, and adjusting one's mental or emotional attitude.

*Extreme emotion places the individual
in reaction mode, which hinders
response time and distorts options.*

Thinking *"I hate Gertrude. She drives me crazy in staff meetings,"* and then doing everything you can to avoid her is an example of strong negative emotion and reaction.

It requires a finer degree of evaluation to determine: "Gertrude dominates the conversation by interrupting and changing the topic before we have completed the agenda. She speaks too loudly. The room is not very large and her voice is high-pitched and sharp." *(Goodness! She sounds horrible. I don't like her either!)*

But now you have the foundation for acknowledging what you don't like in order to develop an action plan and, no, I don't mean getting her fired. You may not be able to "fix" Gertrude, but I believe it is possible to address particular issues.

The next time she prematurely changes the subject, you may point this out and redirect the conversation. Let her know she interrupted you by saying, "Gertrude, I'm sorry, but I hadn't finished my point. Please let me finish." This is better than sitting there quietly fuming while Gertrude runs amok.[6]

Yes, I believe speaking up in a meeting can be thought of as a presentation. To be successful, it is certainly a "performance," one that is most effectively addressed in a proactive mode supported by a clean filter.

The Filter Bottom Line

Enough already! We get it! Our mirrors are smudged and the dirt in our filters cause us to... What exactly?

This is a question for you to answer.

Do your instincts serve you well? Possibly you scrutinize tiny details or stumble haphazardly through your day hoping to avoid confrontations and presentations. Perhaps

---

[6] To allow a personality type like Gertrude to get away with murder is typical, believe it or not, and this "condition" has a name: The Bad Apple Syndrome. Very simply, a group will adjust to the level of the weakest member. For a simple illustration, check out this summary of a research project conducted by Will Felps, PhD, while at the University of Washington: bit.ly/thebadapple

you feel inhibited or maybe you *over*-compensate for challenges that no longer exist.

I offer below two more examples of outwardly successful clients whose neglected filters created professional challenges. I hope these stories help you identify similarities and open the door to your own answers.

Mike

Mike was a very accomplished man, president and co-founder of a successful multi-million dollar company. Yes, he was a busy man. He saw himself as the "My door is always open, I'm just one of the guys" type, but really that sign read, "Hurry up, spit it out because I'm busy."

His "approval rating" with the media as well as his staff was low and his PR firm was hoping I could help.

I noticed that when someone else was speaking, including me (!) he interjected constantly with "Uh-huh," "Yeah," "Oh," etc. These interruptions were incredibly distracting and would have driven poor Mitch (see earlier story) crazy.

I finally asked Mike if he was aware of this habit. He confidently and emphatically answered, "Yes! I think it is a great tool."

I couldn't believe he did this on purpose. "Why?" I asked.

"To hurry others when they speak," he said, "I find that most people talk too slow. No offense, but my time is valuable and I think it helps them get to the point more quickly."

Luckily, I had an instant remedy. I asked Mike to explain something and proceeded to "hurry him along" by constantly interjecting "yeah's" and "uh-huh's."

Mike shook his head and laughed, "Wow! That really is annoying." He stopped.

Sarah

Sarah was an attractive, television news anchor whose energy and upbeat personality made her popular with viewers.

Upon returning from maternity leave, there was a significant difference in her on-air delivery. She changed the way she sat, kept her hands clasped tightly in front of her, and turned only her head when speaking to her co-anchors.

It was noticeable to everyone how uncomfortable and rigid she seemed during a newscast. Even her breathing seemed affected. Viewers began writing and emailing their concerns.

In a private session, she tearfully acknowledged her inability to fit into her pre-baby, size 0-2 suits and was now in a size FOUR!

All of her physical adjustments were designed to hide her protruding stomach. She was being "coached" by a close friend who offered daily critiques. They poured over taped newscasts together looking for bulges and excess fat.

Sadly that story didn't end well and a solution was beyond my scope, but I use it as an example of how obsession with a perceived imperfection can over-shadow and destroy what is natural and healthy.

Joe Cocker made a career out of a voice that would send voice teachers screaming. More than one brilliant person told Barbra Streisand to get her nose fixed and Brooke Shields changed the landscape of eyebrows.

Bottom line?

> *When opening your presence,*
> *it is more productive to move*
> *towards a positive goal than*
> *focus on negative debris.*

Open the Box

To truly appreciate a present, one must remove the wrapping paper, take it out of the box, see it, touch it, and *use it*.

Highly popular vintage toys in pristine, original packaging are incredibly valuable because they are so rare. Let us learn from children, who fearlessly rip into a package, pull out the treasure and begin to play.

My 1962 Barbie© Doll lives in my closet along with her little clothes and accessories. I must have changed her outfits a million times. I explored every micro-inch of that doll; how she bent and where she didn't. I didn't question her limitations. I embraced them and at four-years-old I learned how to put her unbending elbow through a tiny sleeve.

I treasure my Barbie for the very reason that I know her so well. And yes, I might be hundreds of dollars richer today had I chosen to leave her in the box, but the enjoyment and value she brought into my life can never be measured.

Your gifts are to be examined, experimented with and, yes, have fun… Play! Embrace the value of opening a gift.

Exercise
There are four parts in this exercise.

I just described my own Barbie. Are you able to recall a favorite childhood toy? Perhaps it is not a toy, but a sport or activity.

You appreciated its intricacies or simplicity. Its qualities provided almost supernatural significance.

Take a few minutes and write about your "Barbie" and the discoveries made possible through fearless scrutiny and investigation.

Don't put that pen down yet. Now think of the child who played with that favorite toy or participated in the activity you just disclosed. Describe him or her in detail, including the gifts and qualities that contributed to that child's curiosity and self-worth.

Opening, and more importantly, utilizing our innate gifts for the world to see can be a bit intimidating so let's take this slow.

Let's observe someone else. Take a moment to write about someone whose communication style or gifts you appreciate. I encourage you to think of people you know and interact with. You like the way they tell a story. You find them entertaining or amusing. You've never tried to dissect what makes this person a success, so give it a shot. Imagine this person in action. What gifts do these people possess and how do they utilize them? Make sure you analyze voice and appearance while you're at it.

Last, but not least, it only makes sense to spend a little time writing about one person, someone you interact with, whose manner does not appeal to you. Be descriptive. Be objective. This is not about disliking a person, but observing the nuances of ineffective behaviors.

These kinds of observations, both negative and positive, are opportunities. Emulating a quality, trait or style you find appealing is accomplished by acknowledging what is similar (attainable) in yourself.

Likewise, that which invokes negative reactions provides the opportunity to recognize corresponding characteristics.

An interesting thing often happens when we do this kind of scrutiny. We find that the level of perfection to which we hold others is quite different than what we demand of ourselves. In other words, acceptance or rejection of another is rarely tied to the idea of perfection, yet we often prescribe unrealistic measurements of worthiness to ourselves.

I hope this "spring cleaning" has given you a greater appreciation for the importance of developing your personal objectivity. Let me summarize some chapter highlights from before we move on:

- No one sees themselves the way an audience does, but you can clean the mirror to get a clearer image.
- Everyone has a message filter. Sifting through the superfluous clutter makes room for new, empowering options.
- Reacting, compensating and scrutinizing are distractions, not choices. Replacing a distraction with an intention creates positive objectives.
- Opening your presence is directly linked to appreciating your presents, which means using them. Have fun, experiment and play fearlessly.

Next, we'll break down the elements behind face-to-face communication and examine how impressions are formed. Understanding these mechanics empower you to focus when presenting and hone your reception skills for optimum benefit.

Chapter 4. "Gimme an 'A!'"

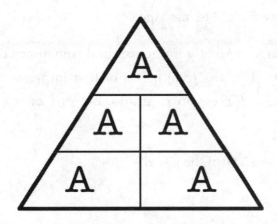

E ach "A" in the above pyramid represents one of five primary factors that are the building blocks for how we form, send and receive messages when standing face-to-face with other human beings.

Volumes have been written on this complex subject, but I believe in keeping things simple.

For the purpose of eliminating debris that gets in the way of you presenting the You that you want others to see, pick an "A," any "A." Look at it. Memorize it. Then stick it back in the deck.

Opening Your Presence

Embrace and improve only that one element of communication and you are that much closer to being a more effective, powerful and, hopefully, genuine you.

These As *are* in order of importance and I will start with the "A" that is the most powerful because it makes an immediate, indelible message.

It is silent, but greatly influences and sometimes determines credibility. It is the foundation of first impressions. This is the hardest impression to un-do, but one of the easiest to adjust.

Any guesses? Turn the page.

Appearance

Yep! Within seconds of meeting, your audience formulates judgments about you. With one look, your **appearance** instantly telegraphs information about:

- Health/Hygiene
- Financial Status/Position
- Knowledge/Authority
- Mood/Confidence Level
- Personality
- Preparedness or lack thereof
- Sense of Propriety (Yes, even in this day and age, propriety plays a role. The level and amount depends on your audience.)
- Age (which implies maturity and experience level)
- Likeability/Approachability

Add it all together and your credibility can be made or broken in the blink of an eye. Yes, your appearance silently telegraphs these messages and more! And while being attractive doesn't hurt, beauty is in the eye of the beholder.

So never, ever under- *or* over-estimate what others find attractive!

I want to be very clear that "appearance" is not about being the most beautiful person in the room. It *is* about being your best representative *for the situation.*

I have never had the privilege of serving on a jury, but I've come pretty close. Most recently, I had a clear picture of a trial's outcome simply by the defense attorney's appearance.

It didn't help that he was late and we had been waiting in a warm, small, windowless room for hours. In he strolled. He was not hurrying, nor apologetic. I had never seen so much bling on a man. He looked more like a music video star with large diamond studs in both ears, numerous gold necklaces, rings, bracelets and probably the biggest watch I'd ever seen. His suit, tie and shoes were all trendy, ill-fitting (too tight) and colorful.

As I looked at my co-jurors-in-waiting, their looks of surprise and disgust were not surprising. Most of these people seemed to be working class, lower to middle income individuals, who were most likely giving up wages to do their civic duty.

Say what you will about trying to be fair and balanced while serving on a jury, this lawyer was not making a positive first impression. If he was looking for sympathy for his client, he was not off to a good start.

You may have heard the expression "Communication is 80% non-verbal."

This percentage often varies depending on who is saying it and I've heard it go as high as 98%, which, if true, would mean we were mental telepathists!

But whatever formula or idea you have heard about non-verbal communication, you should know it is powerful. This theory started primarily with studies conducted and published by the noted psychologist, Albert Mehrabian, PhD,[7] whose theory has been quoted, distorted and watered down many times. His original finding is often referred to as the "7%-38%-55% rule" and simply proposes that face-to-face communication has three elements affecting the likeability of the speaker: verbal, vocal and visual.

He concluded that non-verbal behavior (i.e. facial expressions) account for 55%, tone accounts for 38% of the impression or acceptance of the messenger, which puts verbiage in last place at 7%. Hence, the 7%-38%-55%.

---

[7] Albert Mehrabian is a respected psychologist, currently serving as Professor Emeritus of Psychology at UCLA. His initial findings were published in the late '60s and have since been re-interpreted and expanded upon in various ways.

His studies went much further to explore the concept of conflicting messages. For example, when a speaker's tone does not match his choice of words, the audience is most likely going to have confusion or doubt.

The research went even farther to demonstrate that when the speaker's *behavior* or *non-verbal communication* does not match the verbiage, typically the message receiver is *more* influenced by the non-verbal or visual signals.

In plain English:

> *An audience is more apt to be swayed*
> *by what they <u>see</u> than by what they <u>hear</u>.*

And when the two elements are in conflict, there is confusion. Not an ideal scenario.

In my work, I have personally witnessed and experienced the powerful impact of visual over verbal.

One of my broadcast clients had just won an Emmy for her report on a missing child. In our session, she told me how proud she was of this story and how hard she worked. "I just didn't think my visual appearance would make that much difference when the story was so profound, but I realized how right you are about appearance." She continued, "I received *one* email telling me how moving that report was, but I had *dozens* telling me about the bad hair day I was having!"

In all fairness, I believe the "bad hair" was simply a noticeable distraction as this news anchor was typically seen sitting behind the anchor desk as opposed to outdoors, standing in the middle of a field. TV viewers were accustomed to her studio perfection with hair and make-up meticulously groomed.

Appearance is an important part of the presentation and consistency sets an expectation. Icy snow was a different backdrop and the elements (and hair) could not be controlled.

Visual impressions are made in *fractions* of a second, literally the blink of an eye, and these conclusions may be conscious or completely subconscious, depending on the individual. These impressions are being processed through layers of pre-conceived notions and assumptions. We all have filters and lenses by which we judge the world, and to not appreciate the importance of appearance is a mistake.

I consider the word "appearance" most appropriate because it says it all. How do you appear? *Perception* of reality is the essence of the power behind appearance.

You attend a conference to discuss retirement investments. Who are you more inclined to trust?

I will be the first to admit, the conclusions we draw might be wrong. Either person may make excellent decisions and have a wealth of knowledge and experience. Nevertheless, impressions are made in seconds.

Do you want your audience to work that hard to get to know you? Chances are most won't. And do you want to work that hard to overcome a possibly negative first impression?

If your look impacts the audience's perception of your credibility, you are creating a conflict to be resolved. In time, and it may be quite a bit of time, one's reputation, word of mouth and notoriety will speak louder than appearance, but in new business and first impressions, appearance speaks the loudest.

Your look should support and enhance your message, not distract from it!

The good news is, with thoughtful consideration, you can send a specific message, loudly. Obviously, first impressions and appearance go far beyond what you wear and how you style your hair, but first things first. I am often asked for guidelines[8] on grooming and wardrobe, so here we go.

Wardrobe

How you dress is an outward representation that demonstrates your awareness of the importance of the meeting or presentation and respect for the people you will be addressing.

Below are factors that influence your wardrobe selections.

- **Type of event or situation** (job interview, Tupperware party, black-tie fundraiser…)
- **Venue** (conference room or living room, outdoor arena or supervisor's office)
- **Kind of message** (State of Union, sales, progress report)
- **Time of day** (breakfast meeting or cocktail party)
- **Season** (This may seem obvious, but I saw a female speaker step to the stage in a cotton halter dress in the middle of winter! No, she was not my client.)
- **Professional and socio-economic status of the group**

---

[8] I generally stay away from rules and absolutes (i.e. "always do this," "never do that"). I prefer to make suggestions that encourage clients to embrace their individuality while honoring the situation and ultimate goals. These are indeed suggestions.

To dress accordingly shows respect for your audience, which provides instant credibility.

The three main motivations behind wardrobe selection are:

1. Dress appropriately for the situation and audience.
2. Your "look" should support and not distract from your message.
3. Your wardrobe should not distract *you*!

To illustrate, let me offer up a couple of true stories.

> *A young attorney showed up at an important client luncheon dressed in an old suit that had that "shiny" look from too many cleanings. His wrinkled shirt had a frayed collar and his cuffs were dirty. How do I know this? I heard about it directly from the firm's founding partner, who stood before me in a custom suit, a starched handkerchief in his breast pocket, and platinum cufflinks. It seemed obvious that dress was important to this man, the* <u>employer</u>.

Lesson: Take the lead on dress from your boss.[9]

> *I was totally fascinated by a presentation made by a beautiful young woman who seemed extremely proud of... her belly button ring. (Please note: I have no personal issue or opinion of one having piercings and body art, except when it distracts from the message and the messenger.) She was speaking to a conservative group, mostly men. Her credibility*

---

[9] You may not be able to afford the same designer label or custom tailored couture, but there are excellent substitutions. Know when to discard old, frayed clothing and buy an iron!

came into question and the focus of her audience was on anything but the message. It was just plain distracting to watch her too short, tight blouse move up and down revealing her navel jewelry.

Lesson: Unless you have a talking belly button, a boardroom presentation is not the time to display it.

I have sat through *many* painful presentations by women who are pulling at their too-tight, ill-fitting outfit. Keeping a snug blouse closed, while tugging at a skirt that is too short, does not only distract the audience, but the speaker as well. *No one <u>cares</u> or even <u>knows</u> what size you wear. **Buy what fits.**[10]*

Interestingly enough, men seem to have the opposite problem. I've typically noticed men who have not had their suits tailored, so the pant and sleeve lengths are too long and jackets bag and drape so that they look like they're wearing someone else's suit. It's simply distracting and sends a negative message.

A few easy guidelines:

1. **Err on the side of conservative**. Unless you are in the fashion industry, your first presentation to the new boss is not the time to make a dramatic fashion statement.

---

[10] If you have put on a few pounds and don't want to invest in a whole new wardrobe, select a few items to tide you over. If you have been trying to lose the same 30 pounds for 2 years, get honest with yourself and invest in a realistic size.

2. **Get a full length mirror and use it**. A beautiful suit can quickly become a presentation "don't" with stray threads, stains and irregular hems.

3. **Get educated!** When possible, use a personal shopper. This is their business. If you are not sure of the dress code, find out. Make a phone call, ask a friend, ask Siri. The spotlight is bright, especially when all eyes are on you.

4. **New shoes should not be broken in during a presentation.** If you will be standing for any length of time, this is not the time to wear new shoes. Nothing is more distracting and painful (to the speaker!) than ill-fitting shoes.

Grooming and Make-Up

Men, it all depends on your profession, position, industry, etc., but key words to remember are neat, clean and non-distracting.

Facial hair is a personal call, but again, I emphasize neat. Unruly moustache hairs are extremely distracting in a close conversation and scraggly beards raise the question of cleanliness.

I recently observed two well-dressed men having lunch and the one doing all the talking had a blob of food hanging in his beard. I'm sure he could not feel this but his dining companion (his audience) certainly couldn't miss it!

Hands and even shoes send a strong message. I saw a young man on the streets of New York recently who was the walking billboard for vibrant youth and contemporary style ... his suit was tailored to his physique, his tie was perfect, his hair was hip, yet not overly trendy. And then I saw his shoes. I had never seen a rattier, more scuffed up pair of Italian loafers in my life. It diminished the rest of the look. Grooming applies to shoes too.

Ladies, you may not like the feeling of make-up foundation or "a ton of make-up," as I've often heard it said, but I hope you can appreciate this: when the audience is not looking at your PowerPoint presentation or their phones, the average person is looking you in the eye. In this visual setting, a little color in the cheeks or lips goes a long way toward establishing the message, "I am glad to be here."

I want to make it clear that I am not suggesting you look like Miss America for every meeting. In fact, I've suggested to more than one client that they tone *down* their make-up. However, your "look" should say that you cared enough to put some thought and effort in your appearance.

What does your grooming say about you? I'm not the only one to notice an unwashed face or my favorite, *airplane hair*.

I attended a conference recently where the speaker "confessed" she had just flown in and her plane was late and she had a terrible time getting a cab, blah, blah, blah...

Two observations. First, what a terrible way to begin a meeting! Second, she didn't need to explain because everyone could recognize her airplane hair... and face! Not only was her hair flattened and smashed on one side, but her face was devoid of any color or "grooming."

In speaking with her afterward, I couldn't help but notice little bits of sleep in the corners of her eyes. This woman obviously had not stopped to look in a mirror before speaking to a roomful of executives.

Please make time. I would even say it is better to be a few minutes late than look unkempt. Neither is desirable, but I'm sure very few were able to hear and appreciate this speaker's message. I even overheard a gentleman ask her if she needed a break to "freshen up," that she brushed off as frivolous.

(Hint: If you don't like looking in mirrors, chances are people don't want to look at you either.)

Business travel may seem glamorous to those who do not have to do so regularly, but struggle with delayed flights and missed meetings, eat a hotdog while running down the jet way with a roller bag for the hundredth time and the glamour is minimal. Sometimes arriving at your destination rested, groomed and engaged is a challenge, but always desirable.

If you feel inadequate or lacking in basic grooming skills, make sure you get the right help.

It is like therapy. You have to find a therapist you trust and it may take a few interviews. The department store saleslady with fuchsia mascara is not your only resource. Shop around.

What Meets the Eye

Get the idea that there's more to appearance than what meets the eye?

I hope you can appreciate how important your look is to the success of your meeting, interview or presentation. For an interesting perspective and in-depth examination of the neuroscience and psychology behind messaging that occurs literally "in the blink of an eye," I highly recommend Malcolm Gladwell's book, *Blink: The Power of Thinking Without Thinking*.

Let's move on to the next "A."

This element plays a powerful role in the science of interpersonal messaging and contributes heavily to the first impression. Most people don't realize this, but its real strength lies in how it aids the speaker. Here's a hint... It's not time for words yet. Why? Because **actions** speak louder than words.

ACTIONS

Actions are any physical movements, such as gestures, facial expressions, body language and anything that may diminish or enhance your verbal message.

What you do (how you act) *greatly* affects how the audience receives you. And, get ready... Actions also have an enormous impact on how you sound and feel.

Exercise

Let's do an experiment. Unless you are strapped into a seatbelt or crammed into a crowded elevator, try something for me. Stand up. Think of an event in your life that you are passionate and happy about.

Yes, this should be positive; not about the next door neighbor who keeps driving up over your curb and knocking over your trash cans. This can be your new lawn mower, the birth of your baby or that million-dollar sale.

If you can't think of something specific, that's unfortunate, but try to imagine yourself winning the lottery. *You* have the winning ticket!

Now, tell someone about it. It can be your best friend or partner, either imaginary or real, but do it aloud. Let your passion and excitement flow. Do this for at least 20 seconds. (Even if you are unable to do this exercise aloud, you should be able to imagine yourself in action.) Whew! Do you *feel* some of this passion? Does this other person "see" how you feel?

Can you imagine being able to convey this same enthusiasm without your arms and hands or even a smile?

Likewise, smiling while trying to tell someone you ran over their dog in the driveway (the same person running over your trash cans…) will most likely get you a punch in the nose.

Physically supporting your message
helps the audience "hear."

And

Deep breathing and physical movement
reduce nervous energy.

There is research that explains in great detail the physiological factors behind breathing and its relationship to releasing toxins and helping detoxify the body. Movement stimulates brain chemicals that boost your mood.

The next time you grasp that podium like your life depends on it, realize you are locking in tension that has nowhere to go. The same is true for shoving your hands into both pockets or clutching pens, papers or even that remote clicker.

The three main reasons people give me for not using their hands are:

- I don't know what to *do* with my hands.
- I'm afraid I will gesture too much and look like a fool.
- I don't want people to see my hands shake.

To which I say, "You know what to do with your hands because you do it every day. It is only because you are so keenly aware of being watched that you become self-conscious. In 17 years of coaching, only twice did I see someone gesture inanely or shake so much that it was noticeable."

One more thought to keep in mind the next time you want to keep those hands still.

Gestures help the flow of thoughts and ideas.

I have often noticed that speakers who are stiff or reluctant to gesture are much more likely to lose their train of thought. I've seen countless speakers go blank and instinctively begin to move, either taking a few steps or gesturing, to trigger their memory and most often it works!

Opening Your Presence

Speakers who insist on memorizing or reading from a script are more likely not to gesture adequately. I do a little exercise where I ask my client to pause and then to repeat the same section in their own words, to me and only me. I may move closer or lower my own voice, but it never fails, this same person who seconds before may have sounded artificial or struggled with the idea of what to do with their hands, immediately relaxes and speaks conversationally, gesturing beautifully.

I will talk about this in more detail in Chapter 5, but first, a few tips:

- Smiling, eye contact and using the 43 muscles in your face tell a much better story than trying to look official.
- Give yourself permission to move. Rather than focus on what you don't want to do, tell yourself it's better to move. Believe it.
- How you walk to the podium, address your host, and hold yourself in general speaks *volumes* about your level of confidence. Standing strong also helps you *feel* more powerful.

Take advantage of all the benefits actions provide you and your audience.

And now... it's time to speak.

Audio

Finally! Coming in at third place, we have **audio**, what the audience hears. And yes, what you say is important. It is very important. You have crafted a compelling message. Let's hear it!

But your audience hears more than words. They also hear the tone and vocal nuances adding meaning to those words... If you aren't providing this guidance, they will interpret your message any way they choose, even making assumptions about you along the way. So remember:

*How you say something carries more impact
than what you say.*

Being truthful is important. Facts should be accurate. But you have more power in your manner of delivery than what is in individual words.

If inflection, emphasis and human connection meant nothing, your audience could simply read those handouts. But you want them to know, to understand, that 2% growth in deliverables since February is **huge**! This is more than had been hoped for.

If they simply read 2% or see it on a graph, is that really as powerful as you selling it?

The spirit and tone convey significance. Elements to consider are:

- Inflection
- Emphasis
- Pauses
- Emotional nuance

Let me be clear. Even if this is a status report with facts and figures, you want your audience to feel something or, at least, stay awake. Perhaps the greatest mistake I witness (and I witness it frequently, so pull up a chair) is confusing serious subject matter with the need to act serious.

I often work in corporate environments. When I ask clients to tell me an emotion they hope to convey or the mood of the presentation, the #1 adjective I hear is "serious."

How do you act serious? Try standing before a mirror and "act serious." What does this look like? Does this look like someone *you* want to listen to?

To be taken seriously does not mean you must act seriously.

You don't want to confuse an ideal outcome (closing the deal, making the sale, etc.), which may be serious to you, with feeling you must *act* seriously.

I've been told this was a "serious presentation" only to find out my client was pitching new uniform options! Yes, finding that ideal, cost-effective uniform for your employees is important, as is the weather, a product launch, book deal, skin cream, or animal by-products.

Whatever your industry, it is all important. It is best to take all of that serious energy and use it towards finding the best way to market your product.

Write the Way You Talk

To do justice to an important presentation it is best to write conversationally. Even formal presentations can sound relaxed and in fact may help you convey "heavy" or complex information.

Here are a few general thoughts to help you do justice to the audio element of performance.

- **Talk (write) conversationally, when possible.** Rather than trying to *sound* authoritative, allow your knowledge and experience to speak for you.
- **Be aware of time.** If you are allotted 15 minutes, plan for 12. Most people will run over because they aim

for 15 and wind up with 20, 25, 30; which leads me to...

- **Less IS More.** Less verbiage and minutia means greater retention with the added benefit of you sounding more conversational. The average person remembers a third of what you say. Cram it all in and you sound rushed and feel pressured.
- **Read your script out loud!** The first time you hear these words aloud should not be in front of an audience.

Now Hear This!

To have presentation successes, you must practice, *out loud*.

Whispering at your computer screen so as to not disturb anyone does not do it. You have no idea what you sound like until you do it, so don't let the first time be on the stage.

By all means, prepare! Write. Edit. Use your thesaurus... But at some point you must turn off your computer or put down the pen.

Get on your feet! Practice where it is safe with no interruptions, and use this time to do and act what you may only dream of. Go for it. Be dynamic, use gestures, walk, emote. This simple process will do more for your confidence than any other. It brings into play **Sense Memory.**

Briefly, sense memory is a descendant of affective memory, which is an acting technique introduced by Constantin Stanislavski in his system known as "Method Acting."[11]

Marlon Brando was probably one of the most well-known American method actors. While no one is suggesting you rip your t-shirt and scream "Stellllaaaaa!" in the board room, remember all presentations are a kind of performance.

Sense memory is about your body recalling, almost organically, a past act. The more deeply it is ingrained, the easier or more natural it is to recall. Voilà! When you practice strength, you recall strength. When you practice anxiety and nerves, you reproduce more anxiety and nerves. The best way to avoid this?

Practice. Out loud. On your feet.

And this brings me to the fourth A. So tell me doctor, how do you feel?

The first 3 As (appearance, actions, audio) are *what* you present. The last two greatly influence every choice you make.

---

[11] Constantin Stanislavski was a Russian actor and director, (1863-1934) credited with introducing a disciplined system of acting, the Stanislavski Method, in the early 1900s. This has come to be known as "Method Acting." His methodology was integrated into the Actor's Studio and further developed by great acting teachers, including Stella Adler, Lee Strasberg, Uta Hagen and others.

Attitude

Your **attitude** can be a deal breaker or maker.

Attitude colors the outward projection of internal impulses more than you may realize. If you don't take control of your attitude, it will absolutely control you and color the way you are perceived. Probably the only thing worse than having a bad attitude is not realizing how bad it is.

(Get the feeling this is a biggie?)

It is! Feeling overwhelmed, ill-prepared or unsuitable for the task sabotages presentation success. Feelings of inadequacy, anger, righteousness, fear or superiority are deal breakers. Clenching your fists, barreling through or trying to overcome bad feelings is not the same as acknowledging that which is necessary and most conducive to the success of the mission.

It is absolutely imperative that you embrace the proper attitude and put the focus where it should be; on what you can control and what you want to accomplish.

Of course, the biggest attitude wrecker may be your phobia of any kind of public speaking. To get to the bottom of this or any fear, it helps to take it apart and analyze the pieces.

Let's examine the fear of flying. I'm not a particularly big fan of flying, which is kind of ironic since I do so often. When deciding whether or not to accept my first job as a Talent Coach I had to consider this very real challenge.

I confessed how I felt to a family friend, a pilot, who graciously explained to me that the people's reaction to flying is based in one or more of three basic fears:

- The fear of tight, closed spaces (claustrophobia)
- The fear of heights (acrophobia), which is closely tied to fear of falling
- The fear of strange noises (Ligyrophobia)

My fear of flying is grounded (like that play on words? Flying, grounded?) in the sensation of falling. I mean, I detest and can physically react, if you know what I mean, to carnival rides or fast elevators. This, compounded with my ignorance of aeronautics, and I battled more than one little panic attack. With lots of experience and the help of an authority, I came to have a better understanding of a plane's movements. I have grown to relax and accept flying as a part of my life. I may never *love* it, but I do not fear it.

Opening Your Presence

The same rationale is true with public speaking. When we extract and examine a precise fear, this element can be dealt with. The list of fears in public speaking, as related to me, has been quite varied: the fear of being looked at, falling down, fear of one's boss, fear of not having the answer, stumbling, looking stupid, being judged, hating one's voice, one's hands, one's teeth… the list goes on and on.

And they are all compounded with insecurities created by a lack of understanding of presentation fundamentals. Oh, and don't forget, a lack of practice. Whew!

One reason I love my work so much is watching the light bulb go on as someone "gets it." They move past a fear and I see the weight being lifted. It *is* possible. I see it all the time.

What are you afraid of? What forms your attitude going into a presentation? Are you obsessed about things out of your control? Does this tap into pre-existing fears or is it a lack of experience that prompts your feelings of insecurity.

Exercise

What are your presentation fears, insecurities or dislikes? Be specific.

What simply does not appeal to you about public speaking or addressing co-workers, yet is a part of your job? There may be something you are afraid people will notice or think. Perhaps nothing "scares" you; you're just not a fan. You may feel that something about you is not cut out for speaking... But let's get to the bottom of your presentation attitude.

(Keep writing. I'm going to share a story here.)

Many years ago, when I was a struggling actress and trying to define success for myself, I had to take a long hard look at my finances. A wonderful therapist suggested that I simply start looking at my bank account balance weekly, if not daily.

"Know what's in there – high or low, good or bad – but look at it." Eek! I didn't want to look.

I knew it was bad and what I didn't know couldn't hurt me! Hah! She explained that *not* knowing what you have often creates more anxiety than knowing, even if it is very little. (Thanks Shari!)

When I confessed that I was embarrassed that anyone might know I was in debt, Shari said something profound, "Then don't tell them!"

I took this to heart. I began to budget for what I had. I went on a cash-only basis and in one year I was out of debt. Removing the emotional judgments out of the equation was incredibly empowering.

This may be empowering for you as well. List any "presence" issues you have, that which prevents you from being the master communicator you know lies within. These must be issues over which you have some kind of control.

If for example, you feel your main obstacle is "my boss is a jerk," this must be spun so that you have ownership of the situation: "I do not respect my boss. When I speak in front of him, I make more mistakes because I feel he is scrutinizing my every move. His demeanor intimidates me. His criticisms are harsh and I try to attract as little of his attention as possible."

Based on this statement, you now have options to explore. When you believe that the other person is in control of your actions, you are trapped.

As objectively and unemotionally as possible, look at each item on your personal list and make sure it is worded so that you have responsibility for action. Then ask yourself, "Is this fear based on truth?"

If it is an irrational fear, condition or, as yet, unrealized situation, you are allowing a lie to dictate your success. I do not mean to imply that "Poof! Your troubles will immediately vanish." But looking something in the eye, accepting what is, creates a small shift in attitude that is the beginning of a large turn in action.

For each item, you may also ask yourself, "What would a wise person do?" If an immediate answer arises, write it down, contemplate the action and when the time is right, take that sensible step. One at a time.

Let's put the list aside for now. Even this brief observation will create a mindfulness you did not have before and you may find yourself addressing challenges you once did not know existed.

The Last Minute Upset

Have you ever rushed into a presentation or meeting, having just hung up the phone from an argument with your spouse or child? Maybe you've been going 100 miles per hour all morning only to realize you are 10 minutes late for your meeting and have to grab your notes and run?

Perhaps your attention is still on the last presentation where the PowerPoint slides didn't work and you are afraid it won't work this time either. You forgot to have Tech Support look at the problem and you didn't have time to review it yourself...

When you have spent time generating a powerful frame of mind, even last minute upsets are more manageable.

> *A solid foundation (the right attitude) means*
> *you are better prepared to compensate for*
> *last minute interruptions and upsets.*

This is why it is empowering to spend some of that preparation time on your attitude and intention.

I Got a New Attitude!

Put on some music and dance, because integrating intention and ideal outcome shapes your outlook.

> *Personal intention paves the road to an ideal outcome.*

> *An ideal outcome provides the road map for creating an*
> *exceptional impression or presentation.*

> *Knowing what exceptional impression you want to make*
> *requires attention.*

We will discuss how to prepare and how to allocate your preparation time in Chapter 6, but for now, here is a breakdown of these stimulating objectives.

Ideal outcome answers one or all of these questions:

- What do I want my audience to *do*? For your project (idea, concept, etc.) to succeed, is there an actionable request?
- How do I want them to *feel*? Are you hoping to change their attitude? Actions are predicated on feelings. If what you are hoping for is action, you still want to give attention to the sentiment that inspires the act. Your audience is bound to feel something. Let's make sure it's not bored.
- What do I want my audience to *remember*? I've already mentioned that the average audience member will be able to recall only about a third of your presentation. Make sure it is the third you *want* them to remember.

Intention gives purpose to your actions. It is the motivating factor to address *how* you will achieve the above.

- How will I motivate, excite and prompt action? (What will I say, show and/or do to get them pumped?)
- How, when and where do I elicit emotional responses? Using humor, visual aids, demonstrations and examples are a good start.

- How do I make my important ideas stand out? (Hint: First, you need to know what is most important. Here's another hint. It's not *all* important. Pick!)

Exceptional impression is personal. It is about you.

- What do I want my audience to know or feel about me when I'm done?
- What impressions do I want to make and how do I do this? (Hint: Exceptional impressions are always positive and genuine. If your impression is to be upbeat and approachable, you had better display energy, smile, engage (good eye contact) and speak (write) conversationally.)

The more specific you are, the more you are able to achieve clarity for your audience *and* you! Hence, you feel more empowered – more complete and secure, if you will – at performance time. Answering the above questions will be the foundation for your outline.

I know this may sound like a lot of work, but I promise you, depending on the subject, we are talking minutes of your preparation time.

I have provided two examples below. The first one is for a more formal presentation and the second is for a job interview. I hope you will find concepts applicable to your situation.

Scenario Number One

Don't Tear It Down

Steve, a local architect, wanted to stop the demolition of an old downtown department store (ideal outcome) by having it declared a historical landmark (actionable item).

He was speaking to several civic organizations and businesses to increase awareness and present his ideas for possible use and preservation.

1. Ideal Outcome
    a. **Do**: He wanted his audience to call, visit or write letters to the owners of the building asking for a delay in the demolition and to consider saving it as a landmark building. He also wanted them to spread the word and ask their friends and neighbors to help as well.
    b. **Feel**: Steve believed that to motivate people to action he needed them to care about the building as a living entity. He wanted them to appreciate its beauty, long hidden by boarded windows and barbed wired fences. He wanted them to feel an appreciation for its history and contribution to their town's development.
    c. **Remember**: He needed them to know which building was in question, remember the scheduled demolition date, who to write the

letters to, who to visit, and the ideal date by which to do this.

2. Intention

    a. He decided to open his presentation by showing the store's evolution through a montage of black and white photographs of the store with appropriate music. He made periodic references to momentous occasions in the store's history like the unveiling of the town's first escalator. He had photographs of celebrities who had visited through the years. He personalized this presentation with photographs he had collected that showed young boys buying their first suit, girls getting their ears pierced, and families dressed for a Saturday shopping experience. He also included old newspaper advertisements that evoked laughter. He allowed time for audience members to share personal remembrances and ask questions.

    b. His talk included his ideas for preserving the exterior of the building while creating contemporary condos and office spaces. He had done research and provided positive information for ways this could increase business and revenue for many local businesses.

    c. He ended his presentation by telling his audience exactly what he hoped they would do. He provided handouts with the e-mail, phone and mailing address for the appropriate parties. He provided sample text for the letters.

3. Impression

a. To motivate his audience, he knew his own enthusiasm and passion must show. He warmly greeted his audience as they were seated, and made a decision to mingle and interact with people before and after the actual presentation. He knew it was important that they see him as a member of the community, someone who cared about the future of the town, and not just this one building. He made it a priority to be warm and inviting; to speak conversationally, smile and make great eye contact. He used people's names and made introductions, when possible, to create a larger circle.

b. Following the presentation, Steve did not race away to his next appointment. He scheduled his day so that he was able to mingle and greet interested parties personally.

By understanding exactly what he needed people to do and hoped they would feel, Steve was able to customize his presentation and personalize his delivery style for maximum benefit.

Scenario Number Two

The Final Interview

Beth had her third and final interview for a sales position with a wholesale furniture company. While she had sales experience, she knew little about decorating and furnishings. Her background was in the hotel business, moving up from front desk clerk to sales manager.

After the previous interviews with HR and another Sales Rep, and doing her due diligence on the company, Beth did the following:

1. Ideal outcome (To land the position, Beth extended her focus beyond a "get the job!" mentality to embrace the "do, feel, remember" mentality.)

    a. **Do**: She wanted these prospective employers to see her as a member of the team. She wanted them to appreciate her sales experience and her skill of being able to deal with varying clientele and personalities. She wanted them to be inspired enough to begin the negotiating process before she walked out the door.

    b. **Feel**: She wanted them to feel comfortable with her and appreciate her openness and willingness to learn. She wanted them to feel excited to have her on board and energized by what she would bring to the table.

    c. **Remember**: It was important they know she had a wealth of sales experience and that she was ready to embrace a new industry. She appreciated fine furnishings and felt she had a good flair. Above all, she wanted them to remember *her*.

2. Intention

    a. Beth went prepared with her own questions as well as an exit statement. She knew in the sales world that asking for the sale was important. She asked for the position. She made it clear that she felt she was a good fit and this company was where she wanted to be. Prior to the interview, she researched fabrics and materials used in furnishings. She spoke to an interior decorator friend and asked for a few tips; key buzzwords and aspects of design. She researched other design companies who had similar styles and made a note of what made this company stand out.

    b. Beth knew she needed to make a powerful visual statement as well as intellectually and professionally. So prior to the interview, Beth bought a new outfit. She did not shop at her usual go-to place for conservative suits. She got help from a personal shopper and bought something colorful and fun. This company was

           trendy and she noticed everyone had real style in
           their clothing and manner.

3. Impression

    a. She entered the room with purpose, shook hands firmly while smiling and making great eye contact.

    b. Beth prepared a brief, positive opening statement. She focused on being personable, friendly and confident about her sales experience and record.

What Beth did *not* do, was focus on (apologize for) the fact that she had no experience in selling furniture and that she was not an interior decorator.

I hope you can appreciate how deeply you can dive into formulating your ideal outcome and supporting it by your intentions. The idea is to break up a larger concept into actionable items.

I have seen the positive effects and amazing transformation in speakers by adherence to this mindset during the preparation process. I have devoted Chapter 6 to the concept of how to "package the goods," which focuses on audience benefit. If the audience wins, you win.

"They Call Me Mister Tibbs!"

This is one of the best lines in a movie, ever. When the sheriff of a small, southern town in the '60s asks the African-American, big-shot detective what he's called up there in Philadelphia, Sidney Poitier as Virgil Tibbs responds, "They call me Mister Tibbs!"

This character knows who he is. His approach and manner are related to his attitude about his position.

In regard to presentations, I have often found that one's job title follows the person onto the speaker's platform. This can work well for some or it may act as a detriment.

Here are two scenarios where a preoccupation on position or title may hinder the speaker.

The Administrative Assistant

An administrative assistant is called upon to do a project update for senior-level management. This admin is responsible for compiling and organizing data on a daily basis. She manages the resources, knows all the players, and the parts they play. In this situation, the admin is the authority.

If he or she sees themselves as "only an admin" and is overwhelmed by the audience, everything from vocal volume, dress, body language and demeanor may reflect these feelings.

The CEO

A CEO "asks" his team to participate in a charity benefit for which he sits on the board. His request sounds more like a demand. Many employees would most likely participate out of fear of future repercussions or to be seen as team players, but enthusiasm is low and resentment high. There is a better way...

The speaker or (seller) can find the best attitude by assuming a new position or job title.

Here are some other hats you might want to wear that aid in finding the best intention and impression:

- **Interpreter**. An interpreter translates, explains and clarifies. To go from one language to another, it is important to grasp the meaning and tone as well as strict definition. Embracing your role as an interpreter may help you slow down or enunciate more. You may feel a greater connection to the thoughts behind the words or think in more conversational terms. It may affect how you put your visual aids together. It is an extremely valuable tool for stepping outside of your usual role for greater insight into the message your audience needs to hear.
- **Guide**. A tour guide is used in many settings from museum to Grand Canyon. It is his or her job to lead, direct and guide. You hope to make your audience's

experience as pleasant and helpful as possible. As you put your presentation together, imagine how to lead someone through it as though it were an exhibit at the Metropolitan. Help them "see" the big picture...

- **Host or Hostess/Emcee.** Hosting is about poise, confidence and grace. Acting in an assured, but gracious manner exudes confidence. (Please note I said "acting" as you might not feel assured, but the longer one fakes this attitude, the more real it becomes.) The audience can relax because the host is taking care of it, whatever "it" is.

  Can you imagine a cold, aloof hostess for a charity event? The generosity of donors may be greatly influenced by personal feelings about the host or hostess. *Welcome* your guests into the presentation. *Engage* them for the length of their stay. *Assure* your audience that this will be a pleasure... These are all aspects of a great host and presenter.

I said earlier there is nothing worse than not knowing you have a bad attitude. I will now amend this to offer one factor that might also fit the bill: not caring.

I seldom come across people who do not care, but it happens. For whatever reason, there is nothing that can be said or done that motivates them to better themselves, the cause, or human relations. Even the idea of losing a sale, job or respect, is not a motivating factor, because they don't care.

An attitude that runs neck-and-neck with indifference is the "victim mentality." Everything is beyond their control or someone else's fault. They see no other options because they don't know, understand or are afraid. It becomes simpler to believe that no options exist because then they are off the hook. "Hey, don't look at me. There is nothing I can do."

Believing you have no options means there *are* none.

You always have options… Always, always. They may not be ideal. You may not be crazy about them, but you are able to choose, even when it feels like you are opting for the least of all evils.

I love this quote attributed to Henry Ford.

> *Whether you believe you can do a thing or not,*
> *you are right.*

This brings me to the introduction of our fifth and final "A." But first a quick review of the previous "As:"

- Appearance
- Actions
- Audio
- Attitude

AUDIENCE

Ahhhh... the **audience**. You can't pick 'em and you can't do it without 'em. But you can do your best to clarify the presentation, using the audience point of view as reference.

All interactions are a form of presenting the authentic you. Adjusting to the audience is not about being fake or lying, it's about embracing all of you and tapping into that which is most suitable and powerful *for your audience*.

To return to Concept Number One, you are the seller and the audience is the buyer of your wares. Learn as much about them as possible and adjust accordingly. The buyer holds the cards, the money and, in many ways, the power. So you don't want to make them work too hard to buy into what you're selling. *Why?*

All together now! *Because chances are they won't.*

Would you? How hard do you work to repeatedly shop in a store where items are confusing, over-priced and hard to find? How often would you subject yourself to a disagreeable sales representative?

It may sound like the audience should make you nervous because of the control they seem to have in the situation, but here's what they do not control: they do not control *your* power to make a fantastic impression and positive impact; your ability to speak with conviction, energy and enthusiasm, to set a tone, paint a picture, convey authority and knowledge... But all of these elements work best, when you *embrace* who you are talking to. This is where **attitude works to synchronize your efforts** in harmonious balance.

You cannot resent your audience and appeal to them. You cannot avoid or perform a disservice to your audience and think you will win.

Doing your due diligence means knowing as much as possible about the audience and the venue. Areas to explore include:

- Industry
- Position or job title
- Level of expertise or familiarity in *your* subject matter
- Socioeconomic backgrounds
- Audience size
- Venue location and size. (Are you meeting at your client's country club, hotel bar, construction site, or at

a coffee shop? Outdoor arena, noisy bistro or intimate board room?)

All of the above are valuable clues that lead you to a more positive outcome.

With appreciation for your audience, combined with knowledge on the subject and understanding of your ideal outcome and intentions, you wield a powerful sword.

I'm going to mention one last, important aspect of your audience that many clients seem to forget. In the rush to make a point, stand out, win, succeed, get noticed, be an authority, people forget that they are speaking to other human beings.

Your audience is not filled with objects, these are people. And before you say, "Duh! Does she think I'm stupid?" let me say that the most powerful element of an impactful impression is emotional.

Making a human connection requires being a person, not a robot. This entails listening and responding as well as talking. This means letting go of the idea of perfection.

Accept yourself, the situation and your audience.

Well, that sounds like a 6TH A...

I know, I know. I said there were five and now I'm throwing another one at you. But it's nothing new. I've mentioned it before and now it is official. Accept! Your new pyramid will look something like this:

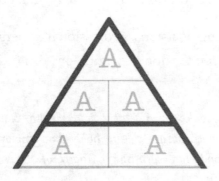

Accept limitations, but *embrace* your strengths.

I can hear you now:

"OK, I accept the fact that I'm shy… I'm a huge pushover without a backbone and people walk all over me. I accept it. OK? I SAID I ACCEPT IT!"

Uh, that's not acceptance.

In *Daring Greatly* by Brené Brown, PhD, Dr. Brown writes:

> We humans have a tendency to define things by what they are not.

I find this incredibly true. Many clients readily tell me what they are not. They list their challenges, faults, burdens, what they hate and can't seem to master. But when asked what makes them excellent, they struggle to find the right words.

At the root of this is the tendency to make comparisons. "Ted does this and I don't, therefore he must be 'right.'"

Wrong. Making decisions, professional or personal, based on what we aren't, don't want, or can't accept is not empowering.

I recently spoke to a Fitness and Health Club marketing team. Their corporate culture holds that employees use the facilities and, not surprisingly, many of these people are incredibly fit.

Here's what I am not: an authority on fitness. I am not a gym rat and certainly not the skinniest person in the room. I eat well and live a healthy lifestyle. Honestly, I've struggled for most of my life with food and body imaging, and here I was speaking to fitness experts. I had a month to prepare.

I didn't "react" by starving myself or running to the gym 50 times hoping to get skinny before the workshop. (Believe me, there was a day when I would have done exactly that!) I did not focus on what I am not, but made sure that the best looking me walked onto that stage.

Here's what I chose to do: I used analogies when possible, like comparing a presentation warm-up to warming muscles before a workout. I was conversational and sometimes humorous. We analyzed ways to approach and interest busy professionals. Understanding that their typical audience was not fitness people, but people like me, was useful to them and me!

Yes, at the end of the day there may have been someone who judged my size 12 body, but if I had dwelled on feeling physically inadequate, the day would have gone a lot differently.

I am not asking you to rejoice in a frustrating situation. You don't have to love it or even like it. When you accept yourself, others, the room and the situation, and do so with as *little emotion as possible*, you have power.

Accepting your small voice empowers you to ask for a microphone. Accepting your audience gives you the power to custom-design a presentation. Accepting your time limitations, allows you to plan for eliminating minutia. Every second that you wish something wasn't so, you have wasted time and energy. And do we really have that much time to throw away?

Exercise

If you have been playing along, you have described yourself to a police sketch artist and you analyzed your voice.

Now, we'll focus on the qualities that you project at home, in the office, or in an actual presentation. Think of this as your own performance review.

It should answer the question: "What do I hope people say

about me when I am not around?" (If you think people don't have an opinion of you or don't talk about you when you're not around, call me. Really... We should talk.)

We're looking for qualities. This is what you *hope* they say. I've listed some adjectives that I hear frequently. You might want to try the exercise before you look at this list, but either way, go for it.

Professional	Realistic	Productive
Calm	Idealistic	Engaging
Secure	Romantic	Warm
Intelligent	Creative	Friendly
Efficient	Unique	Encouraging
Motivated	Unpredictable	Nurturing
Approachable	Fair	Frank
Genuine	Responsive	Tactful
Pragmatic	Alert	Blunt

The next question to ask yourself is: "Does what you *hope* people will say match what they are really saying?"

Is this the description you currently deserve or is it still a dream? Well, get ready, because I believe we can make that dream a reality.

Chapter 5.   Let's Strap on the Tool Belt

Imagine having a home improvement project in mind and receiving a power drill for your birthday. This is the instrument you need to complete your project! Of course, it would be most helpful if you actually knew what you were doing and understood how a power drill operated and which attachments do what.

Depending on your level of carpentry competency, you may still need to refer to the instruction manual and it wouldn't hurt to have a detailed plan for executing even the simplest of projects.

My point? There is a big difference between being able to pick a drill out of a line-up and having a working understanding of what it can do.

The same thing can be said for scissors. My mother made me think that even walking with scissors in my hand would cause me to lose an eye, but in the hands of my hairdresser they are objects to revere.

All of your communication tools are familiar to you and readily available. I would like to give you a greater appreciation for what they can do when you embrace their true power.

In this scenario, *you* are the craftsman, so let's take a look inside that tool box and make sure we have everything we need to accomplish our task.

These are the tools of the trade.

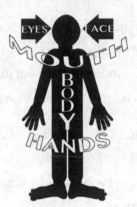

Mouth

Face

Eyes

Hands

Body

Disappointed? Hoping to hear some secret weapon you didn't know you had? Wielded by the informed and practiced person, these *are* weapons to behold.

These tools do not rely on the internet, electricity or batteries. They do not lose their power (without your knowledge or permission), fail to show up or disappear.

The only challenge will be your decision in how to use them. Let's see if you really know the functions and intricacies of each.

Mouth

An awful lot comes out of that mouth, and I don't just mean words. *How* you choose to express or flavor those words creates a stronger message than what you say. So bear with me...

The mouth is like the Swiss Army knife of communication. There are a multitude of attachments. Let's take a closer look.

Volume. I love the episode of Seinfeld where Kramer is dating the "low talker" and Jerry winds up wearing the puffy pirate shirt on the Today Show. This all happens because no one can understand the low talker who never speaks above a whisper.

Are you constantly being asked to repeat yourself? If you think this is frustrating, switch places with the person who cannot hear!

You may be a loud talker. Does your voice make people take a step back? I believe there are instances when a little volume may be necessary to get someone's attention. Make sure you can be heard and understood.

Volume affects the *quality* of a voice, making it more or less pleasant or melodic, especially for women. For a while the trend I noticed most frequently was women who spoke louder than what was normal to gain attention or seek leverage in a mostly male environment.

Recently I have found more and more women speaking in a softer, but guttural way, giving their voice a gruff, fluttering sound. I have found that this style even has a name, "vocal fry."

This has been popularized by certain celebrities doing the "fry" and has been so embraced within some socio-economic groups as to be found positive and desirable.[12]

I hope that it's a trend that goes the way of the Valley Girl sound of the '80s.

Pronunciation and Enunciation. Pronouncing words correctly, especially proper names, goes a long way toward establishing credibility.

There is a street in New Orleans that is spelled B-u-r-g-u-n-d-y, pronounced "bur-GUN'-dee." Every local knows it is not pronounced like the wine and hearing an inexperienced news reporter say "Burgundy" (like the wine) creates a chink in his armor of credibility.

These seemingly small errors build up over time. Pronouncing someone's name is incredibly important and

---

[12] Here is an in-depth article on vocal fry in The Atlantic magazine: bit.ly/womenandvocalfry.

I've learned to detect a telemarketer call in a second when I hear that slight hesitation and then, "May I speak to Mrs. Mule-er?"

First, I'm not a "Mrs." and, second, it is not pronounced that way. Click.

Enunciating clearly (not mumbling) so that you are easily understood is vital. There is nothing more annoying than asking someone to repeat something and have it said in exactly the same way. If I had been able to understand it the first time, I would have!

Try something different, especially if this is a pattern.

Rate or Speed. Are you a *fast* talker? Or are you so slow that people snap their fingers or interrupt to "help" get you to the point?

Cultural and regional styles exist too, so I have no particular recommendation other than make sure you are understood.

I have a girlfriend (*yes, Donna, I'm talking about you*) and that girl is some kind of fast talker. Sometimes her energy and enthusiasm make it hard for her to slow down, but her diction is amazing. I've often thought she could make millions recording those disclaimers at the end of pharmaceutical commercials.

What is considered "normal" in terms of rate of speech varies greatly. Being aware of patterns and *varying* your speed leads to better pacing.

Pacing. This is *how* you use rate or speed. If you have even a mild understanding of music, rate would be the time signature or beat and pacing would be the combination (variation) of notes: quarter notes, half notes, eighths, sixteenths, which receive a longer or shorter allocation of time.

All of this we do naturally in daily life, but start reading or reciting by memory, and the beat becomes sing-songy with little variation.

Parents do well to use this tool when reading bedtime stories as it creates an almost hypnotic spell and sends children to sleep. It is not a compelling delivery style though if you want your audience to remain awake.

Pauses. This simple, seemingly insignificant tool is often left out of the tool belt. In the context of presentations, pausing is an instant attention grabber (if not over-used) and conveys confidence.

It can literally grab your audience by the collar to silently communicate "Prepare yourself, something's up."

Musically, this is a "rest."

Inflection. Since we are talking music, inflection embraces the highs and lows of notes (i.e. moving up and down the scale, Do Re Mi Fa So La Ti Do...).

Even tone deaf people have a sense of the way Julie Andrews works the scale when singing the "Do Re Mi" song in "The Sound of Music."

An example of a monotone voice is the teacher played by Ben Stein in the movie "Ferris Buehler's Day Off." As the character takes attendance, he says, "Buehler? Buehler?" over and over exactly the same way.

Mr. Stein has gone on to use his quirky voice and expression-less face to his advantage in movies, television and writings. This monotone sound creates the very charm behind his iconic delivery.

However, what works for Mr. Stein does not necessarily mean I recommend it. Famous individuals quite often get away with and even exploit the very elements I help clients address.[13] Fame is an amazing antidote for the common ailments of the less renowned.

Emphasis. "It's important to put the *em-PHA'-sis* on the right *Sy-LAH'-ble*." How, where and when you add

---

[13] To name a few: Larry King's suspenders, Donald Trump's hair, Jack Nicholson's sunglasses, Bob Newhart's stutter. The basis for first-time impressions are quite different from famous people's eccentricities.

emphasis increases or diminishes the significance or meaning of what you're saying.

We naturally add emphasis in numerous ways, but when reading (or reciting) the most common form of emphasis is single-word punching.

This is why teleprompter readers often sound artificial. For the record, it is my least favorite form of delivery as it is the least conversational.

Whew! We are still talking about what comes out of your mouth and we haven't even touched upon your other tools yet. I hope you can appreciate the power and flexibility of the mouth. And the moral of this story?

Practice out loud!

All of these elements may be sitting right in that tool box and are gathering dust from underutilization. As we go along, make note of how one tool often works in conjunction with the other.

For example, when I have a client who talks like Mr. Stein and is rather monotonic, what tool do we work with first? Well, it's not the voice so stay tuned and you'll find out.

The next tool you'll want to take out of the tool box is...

Face

Yes, you have a multitude of facial expressions and when your face and voice work in conjunction, you are a powerhouse!

With almost 50 facial muscles sending all kinds of messages to your audience and six fundamental, universally accepted emotions (happiness, sadness, surprise, fear, anger and disgust), some studies say we are capable of making thousands of expressions.

And those are the involuntary ones. Imagine once you put your mind, er, I mean, *face* to it!

Unless you have nerve damage or a rare condition known as Mobius Syndrome, which inhibits facial expressions, you have the ability to *sell* an idea with your face.

Facial expressions greatly affect the sound and mood of the voice, so if you guessed "face" for my previous question about what tool most affects vocal tone, ding, ding, ding, you win!

It is practically impossible to sound warm without smiling and just try sounding angry. Likewise, you cannot sound angry or even firm if you do.

This is not an official exercise, but you might want to record yourself saying something really negative (for example, "you look horrible today"), but smile while you do it. Your voice will never reflect the corresponding attitude.

Likewise, tell your significant other they look beautiful, but frown while you are doing it and you will most likely get a sarcastic "thanks" (or worse) in return.

Your face has a major impact on your ability to sound convincing. So, get these two in line and not only do you *look* engaged, but you sound it too.

Tool #3 is an attachment to the face, but has special import and thus stands alone.

Eyes

Perhaps you've heard "Eyes are the window to the soul." Or "The eyes say it all."

There is truth in both statements. Salesmen are taught from day one, "Look your customer square in the eye when you firmly shake their hands."

Yes, this is a good rule, but the power of eyes goes way beyond that.

Exercise

This is a quickie and involves no writing, so no excuses!

The best place for this particular exercise is your bathroom mirror. Hold a small towel over the bottom half of your face and smile. What do the eyes say? Are they smiling too?

Try sending a message using *only* the eyes. The rest of your face cannot be seen. Try it. Show that you are frustrated, sad, elated, confident...

If you cannot see it in your eyes, neither can your audience. You must *feel* it in your eyes; by that I mean the eyeballs, not the eyebrows. Eyebrows are great. They frame the eye. But too often people widen their eyes. Raised eyebrows only serve to make you look surprised or awake.

The eyes are the foundation of likeability, warmth, connection and approachability. Eyes are the window, the portal and the key to great connection. The truth is in the eyes.

We've already mentioned the fourth tool, its power and the many uses. Let's give a round of applause to...

Hands

"What do I do with my hands?" is by far the number one question I hear.

Opening Your Presence

A great disservice to your presentation is to try to force your hands into being still, since you most likely gesture every day. Your daily interactions are a form of practice and it is counter-productive to stop what you do regularly just because the venue may be new.

Controlling your hands in a formal presentation is like practicing daily for a marathon and then choosing to run with your hands behind your back. Gestures add meaning and emphasis to your message.

For the speaker, they support physical energy, help thoughts flow, assist with pacing, and release anxiety. This is a powerful tool.

A few notes on beneficial gesturing:

- The most powerful gestures are approximately chest level and can be felt in the shoulders.
- Presentations typically inhibit or exaggerate a speaker's emotions so that normal gestures feel bigger than they are. Warming up and even over-gesticulating during the rehearsal/warm-up process increases your chances of hitting the right level when the pressure is on. (It helps your sense memory, which I talked about in Chapter 4.)
- Very few people gesture too much, but I do see random or meaningless gestures. These are repetitive movements that may feel good but are simply

physical impulses, either a result of one feeling pressured to "do something" or a rhythm/time keeper, much like a choir director. It does nothing for the audience, except perhaps distract, but gives the speaker a false sense of security.

- Script preparation and rehearsals are valuable opportunities to improve gesturing. Highlight important ideas and transitions in your script and then practice in front of a mirror. If this seems foreign to you, start without the mirror, gain confidence and then move to the mirror, or video tape yourself. Yes, you should watch it.
- Lastly, gestures help your audiences see what you mean while releasing nervous energy. It's a win-win proposition.

Last, but not least, our fifth and biggest tool...

Body

Yes, we all have body language and it sends out messages. I don't believe that every time you cross your arms you look disconnected, but I do believe how we hold ourselves conveys powerful clues about energy and confidence.

Body language speaks loudly the minute you are visible. This is one reason I believe the presentation starts the second you enter the room. Once the doors open, you are "on" and the impression has begun.

Opening Your Presence

People who stand up straight and walk in a confident manner, send out positive signals of assurance. Someone who slumps and drags… This isn't rocket science.

What you may not realize is that how you use your body is not only part of the visual message you send, it is what your body can do for, or against, you.

 Exercise
Stand up, please. (You didn't know you were going to do so much exercise reading a book, did you?)

Hunch your shoulders, bend slightly at the waist, and take a big, deep breath. Difficult to do. Unless you allowed your body to instinctively straighten on the inhalation breath, as this is what is necessary for the diaphragm muscles to support lung expansion.

Now, stand up straight, shoulders back, hand on tummy, inhale with a big, expansive breath. Your hand should be gently, but noticeably, pushed forward because, ladies and gentlemen, those lungs expand when they are filled.

A common, physical symptom of anxiety is shortness of breath. Nervousness typically creates tension and tension restricts breathing. Voilà!

There will come a day when you need those big breaths (just ask Shelley Winters in "The Poseidon Adventure") and, like any muscle, the diaphragm needs strengthening.

Exercise

If you do this next exercise, email me! I will give you a gold star and a mention in my next book![14]

Lie on the floor and place the heaviest book (typically a dictionary, if you still own one!) on your tummy and upper abdomen.

Inhale deeply and focus on the abdomen expanding and pushing that book upward. Hold for 10 seconds or so and then, as you exhale, maintain the book in the "up" position. Do not lower it as your lungs decrease in size with the release of air.[15]

When done regularly, this is a form of "sit-up" designed to increase breath awareness and strength of the diaphragm muscles.

---

[14] I'm kidding. But this exercise is incredibly effective and very few people actually do it. If you have breathing troubles, please give it a shot.

[15] Ladies, please notice that when you wear your skinny jeans and you "suck in" to raise the zipper you are actually sucking in your tummy on the inhale. I have worked with so many women who have trouble allowing the lungs to expand on the inhalation because sucking in our tummies is so ingrained.

Other Tools of the Trade

I love graphics, handouts and PowerPoint presentations as much as the next person, but there may come a day when it is you and the audience. A quick example...

During a power outage, WSLS-TV in Roanoke, VA, decided to continue their broadcast from the parking lot using generator power and hand-held cameras.

Keeping their viewers informed with up-to-date weather was important, so armed with only paper and markers, and assisted by the news anchors, the meteorologist told a weather story, literally. This is one of the most popular, still-talked-about broadcasts in that community. This team did not focus on their losses, but the well-being of their viewers. Without any of the usual computer graphs, teleprompter or video, the anchor team continued the newscast, keeping their viewers updated, without losing credibility, and probably gaining respect.

You can see a part of this broadcast on YouTube (bit.ly/WSLSoutside).

Never forget that the power in the PowerPoint software is you. Great communication lies with your ability to connect with your audience as a human being first.

Why? Because people buy *you* before they buy your product.

Another Exercise (Already)

Remember the three people whose delivery or communication style you really appreciate? Hopefully, you wrote them down back in Chapter 3.

Write each name and under each name list Mouth, Face, Eyes, Hands and Body.

Spend a little time visualizing each of these elements. You might remember something you've noticed in the way this person smiles or uses their hands, face or eyes. Close your eyes and "hear" their voice. Possibly they are soft spoken and it is this very quality that entices you to lean in and drink up every drop.

Describe what you notice in as much detail as you can about and why it appeals to you.

Keep going… With Mouth, Face, Eyes, Hands and Body as your guide, think about *yourself*.

Which is your strongest asset? Which do you favor and use the most? Which could use some fertilizer and which needs a little weed killer?

Your Next Step

Okay! We have examined *how* messages are received and *what* (the tools) we use to send them. It's time to look at the entire package.

Chapter 6. Packaging the Goods

U p until now, the spotlight has been on you, the presenter (remember, people buy you before they buy your product) and how you use your personal gifts to relate to the people before you.

Let's shine that light on the product, your message, and the elements that provide color and dynamics to capture your audience's attention.

Up until now, I have referred to your message as a product, which remains true, but we will now add the dynamics of storytelling and how best to unfold the plot. Your presentation is not a "whodunit" where the murderer cannot be revealed until the end.

Factual, business-centered presentations work best when you grab your audience at the beginning, peak their interest with a description of what is to come and what they may expect, and then reveal the story. Think of the presentation more like a book's dust jacket description than the book itself.

Opening Your Presence

You may also think of it as a film's preview. Ever sit through a trailer while waiting for the feature film to begin and feel like you've seen the whole movie? That's what you're aiming for. These people do not have time for the whole movie, they want as complete a version as possible as long as it doesn't take too long.

Keeping with the movie trailer analogy, these productions have almost as many people working on them as the movie itself. That's a slight exaggeration, but a whole lotta planning goes into a great trailer and you need to do the same.

I realize you don't have that kind of time to plan, so to keep things simple and applicable, I offer five basic design elements for you to consider when preparing a speech or presentation.[16]

- Research
- Script/speech development
- Visual aids (PowerPoint slides, handouts, etc.)
- Rehearsal/Delivery
- Personal imaging (wardrobe selection, grooming, etc.)

[16] In this context I am speaking of the more formal presentation, but these principles may be applied to job interviews, interactions with your boss, co-workers and less formal interactions as well.

How much time you spend on these and how you prioritize them is your decision and may vary project to project. In my experience, I find that many of my clients need guidance in order to maximize their time and reap the benefits.

They are making every effort to put together the best presentation possible (I certainly don't believe anyone spends time trying to create a bad one), but I believe time and efforts can be spent more judiciously.

Below is a pie chart to illustrate a typical scenario. Please note that preparation time may be 30 minutes or it could be three months. Each pie slice represents the average *percentage* of total preparation time.[17]

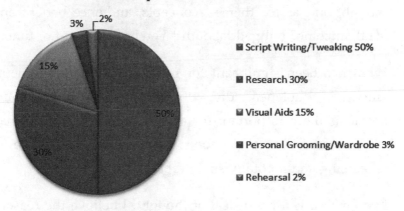

Average Preparation Scenario for Busy Professionals

- Script Writing/Tweaking 50%
- Research 30%
- Visual Aids 15%
- Personal Grooming/Wardrobe 3%
- Rehearsal 2%

---

[17] This is completely unscientific and simply my own illustration of personal observations. Perhaps it looks familiar.

Let's say you indeed have 30 minutes to prepare an impromptu speech that will last 10-15 minutes long.

Seems like no big deal... The average person might spend the majority of that time making notes and bullet points or some kind of "script." Any residual time is given to fact checking, perhaps a handout or quick visual, *maybe* a look in the mirror, and then dashing into the conference room.

Even if the speaker has *months* to prepare for a big presentation, I have found that the extra preparation time doesn't change anything. The presenter's primary focus is still on the information and how to get it all in. The extra time is given to fancier visual aids and slides that are more complex and perhaps have more verbiage.

But time committed to delivery and rehearsal is an afterthought and as for themes, concepts, audience benefit and ideal outcome? Fuhgeddaboudit! You have run out of time.

What has been significant for me is speaking with clients who agree wholeheartedly with the idea that *how* something is said is more important (or at least more impactful) than *what* is said, yet they don't devote significant time to rehearsing and mental/visual preparation.

I've given this a great deal of thought. I believe the reasons vary from not knowing *what* to do or how to do it to not appreciating the efficacy of rehearsal and feeling just plain silly.

I propose two challenges. First, spend just 15 minutes of your total prep time on the elements I described in Chapter 4 (ideal outcome, intention and purpose). See if you need less writing time *and* gain confidence in your skills as a communicator.

My second challenge centers on the rehearsal process. If you currently do not allow time for getting on your feet and practicing the way you want the words to sound in performance, I ask that you give this another 15 minutes. (Or less, depending on how much prep time you have available.)

Let me be clear. If you are sitting there smug in the fact that *you* rehearse, *you* read that script "aloud" *several* times... I want to clarify that it does not count if you do this while sitting at your computer screen, reading silently to yourself. Whispering does not count either.

If you sit in a cubicle style area and you are trying to be courteous to your suite mates, move. Go somewhere else, because a truly beneficial rehearsal means getting up on your feet and speaking aloud so that someone within 20 feet can hear you. This typically means finding a room with a door so you have privacy and do not feel foolish if people see you through the large glass window preening and waving your arms.

In other words, commit to an authentic practice, the kind that improves performance and requires some planning, a little effort and one giant step out of the comfort zone. You will take a giant step into the confidence zone, I guarantee.

We are going to re-configure that preparation pie. Not only will the slices be a little more uniform, but I'm adding a couple of ingredients. Really they are subsets of existing elements, such as specifying "salt, pepper and garlic to taste" in a recipe instead of "seasonings." With this in mind, here is your new pie chart.

New and Improved Preparation Methodology

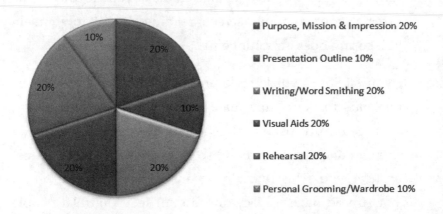

- Purpose, Mission & Impression 20%
- Presentation Outline 10%
- Writing/Word Smithing 20%
- Visual Aids 20%
- Rehearsal 20%
- Personal Grooming/Wardrobe 10%

To make a truly good pie, you start with the end in mind. What kind of pie you are making?

This is an Audience Benefit-pie. It is not the Update Pie or Sound-like-a-Knowitall-Pie. It is designed for maximum audience benefit. That starts with knowing your intention, ideal outcome and impression.

They sound similar but, really, these are three very specific ingredients intended to create the best audience benefit.

I have already touched on this in Chapter 4, but this is how we put those concepts into action.

(And yes, I think you should write it down.)

Here is the scenario. You led a yearlong project developing a new system for addressing customer complaints in a manner that is timely, cost-effective, satisfies customers' expectations, and provides valuable internal data for your company to avoid similar problems in the future.

It is time to unveil the new system and begin a company-wide training program. This all begins with your presentation to the Team Leaders who will then educate their team members and so on.

Let us define your intention, ideal outcome and impression.

- **Your intention gives you purpose.** To fully realize your purpose, it is best to understand "why?" Why is the presentation necessary, relevant or important... to the audience. Not, why is it important to you! We know why it's important to you. You put your blood, sweat and tears into this project, dadgummit! You already understand the significance through your work. Therefore, you have an appreciation for application to a new system. Asking why something is important may seem pretty basic, but you want to dig deeper and move beyond "The purpose is to present/explain X-Y-Z." Why speak?[18] Why not have everyone read a memo? A better statement is: "Because our current methodology is inadequate and we need *full engagement* by *all* team members to make this successful for both the customer and internally. It is important they understand why these changes were necessary, why they need to make full commitment, so that everyone is cognizant of its improved efficiency, efficacy and cost savings."

- **Ideal outcome is your mission**. If the above reasoning is true, what is it going to take to gain your audience's trust and move them to the right course of

---

[18] Even if you have no choice in the matter and this presentation is more of a command than a request, you can find a higher purpose.

action? You must move past the informational stage into motivation and emotion. Let's review.

- How do I want my audience to *feel*?
- What do I want them to *do*? (If you have an action in mind, most likely you need to generate a corresponding emotion. Feeling and doing often work hand in hand.)
- What do I want them to *remember*? (When you are focused on the audience, you are less focused on your fears and thus you have a strong foundation for a new attitude.)

"My mission is to excite these managers to enthusiastically embrace and execute the new system. My mission is to educate and train fully so that these managers are able to teach and excite their team members quickly. My mission is to highlight the 5 steps needed to complete the customer satisfaction survey."

- **Impression is about you.** Intention is shaped by the personal goals based on professional purpose *and* the personal impression you want to create. This helps you remember *why* you, and *how* you will present what you think best tells the story in the order you choose. It means caring what your audience thinks... not only of the material, but about you and being responsive to their needs. This provides the foundation for an action plan. You have already answered the feel, remember and action questions. Now it's time to decide how you will accomplish this. "I will convey great confidence in the plan, be enthusiastic and energetic, and show my strengths as a leader. This means listening and responding to their questions and needs. I want to smile, be approachable and open for questions, yet authoritative. Materials should be clear and concise; not too wordy. I will focus on basics. The details will come in time."

All of the above will most likely not change one bit of information. Content is content, but it provides a strong foundation for creating a powerful performance.

You might be surprised by how difficult it is to step back from a project in which you made such an investment of time and energy.

Deciding what's important *to the audience* can be tough when it *all* seems so important to you. Stimulating your audience, motivating them, keeping their attention and, yes, even informing them is quite a different matter than giving the facts.

In this chart, the steps are in the order I suggest, although you may skip around. However, before you do anything, please spend time on understanding the audience benefit and your ideal outcome.

Next, I highly recommend you jot down a brief outline for the entire presentation. Being the nice person I am as well as someone who loves food analogies, here is a sample outline:

1. Great Opening.
2. Lot of good stuff that is up to you.
3. Powerful Closing.

I call this outline "The Open and Close Sandwich," because great sandwiches are personal. There is always some kind of bread, but the filling is up to you.

Remember, your outline will always include a Great Opening and Powerful Closing. Nailing these two elements will create a positive first *and* last impression.

The Great Opening accomplishes several things. It:

- sets the tone and mood.
- grabs their attention.
- tells your audience *what to expect*.
  (When you are able to set expectations in terms of what will be accomplished and the period of time you need, you are getting on their good side right off the bat.)
- provides *immediate* insight into the speaker.

Opening Your Presence

This is an example of a *not*-great opening:

"Hi, as you all know, like Dave said, my name is Greta, and I was asked to tell you about sales protocols. So let's just get started. The handouts are coming in a second, aren't they? Does anyone know where Beverly is?"

Take the previous idea and scripted, it becomes:

> *Good morning, everyone. I want to thank Dave for asking me to lead this morning's discussion and clarify our new sales protocols. I know you all have a lot of questions about your new quotas and by the time we finish here, in 45 minutes or so, I expect to have addressed these concerns and established a platform for your out-of-town sales calls.*
>
> *I'm excited about the progress we've made, but I'm also aware that this is a work in progress. I want to hear from you. Please, if you have questions[19] as we go along, get my attention.*
>
> *I am also available immediately after this session if we want to move into the other room for coffee and continue the conversation. I know some of you have to leave, but Beverly has my calendar, check with her and make an appointment.*
>
> *Making sure you have everything you need to succeed is my top priority.*
>
> *Everyone comfortable? Great! Beverly is passing out your new packets and I'd like you all to turn to page one.*

---

[19] Raising your hand while telling your audience you welcome questions is a silent but effective way to let your audience know that this is the best way to get your attention.

This opening is not a show-stopper full of comedic brilliance, but it's all there: it's conversational, warm and demonstrates your authority and sincerity. It provides the topic, length of time for the presentation, sets a tone, allows for questions, etc. It conveys that you are in control and yet, you have their best interests at heart. People feel safe, taken care of and appreciated.

One of the other most important parts of your presentation is the closing. This is your last and lingering impression, and it needs to be pretty good, so why not go for powerful.

Here is an example of a *not*-powerful closing:

"Well, thanks everybody, that's about it. Any questions?"

Ugh! And I hear that one so much I'd like to scream.

I've sat through so many creative, wonderful presentations and then hear that at the end. Really?! Aside from the fact that it does not leave the audience with a particularly powerful impression, it basically assures you that there will be no or few questions.

A powerful closing:

- summarizes the key points.
- encourages questions and interaction (when applicable).
- leaves the audience with a positive impression of the speaker and presentation.

Opening Your Presence

Using the same scenario as the above opening, a more powerful closing would sound something like this:

> Thank you so much for your attention this morning. I know we covered a lot of material. I can't tell you how much I appreciate all the input and participation.
>
> The success of this project is in your hands. I want to make sure you have everything you need to be a success, individually and with your teams. So please use your resources. You have several online options as well as a call center.
>
> And if you still feel unsure or have a question, I am available any time. In fact, I will be meeting with you individually to see if you have any more questions or suggestions, so please make sure you get on my calendar.
>
> I have a few minutes left for questions, so if we need to review our immediate steps or anything in particular needs clarification, let's spend the remaining time on what is most important to you.

I'm sure you can hear the difference. If there are a few questions and a bit more discussion you will have to either conclude the meeting at some point or introduce the next speaker.

A second powerful close sounds like this:

> Wow! Those were some great questions and I appreciate the input.

I've taken up enough of your time, so please speak to me privately or email me. We'll meet up again on this subject in another month. Thank you.

Now that you have an idea of a great opening and powerful closing, how are you going to fill the center of this sandwich?

Here are a few hints for putting together your story:

- **Make an Outline.** There should be a beginning, middle and end to this story, not to mention a point! Your opening sets the tone and prepares the audience for what is to come. The middle includes all the pieces that come together for the happy ending. Think narratively; unfold the elements. If the audience cannot understand Point C until they have heard Points A and B, then by all means give them A and B. However, don't get caught up in minutia. Think broad swipes. Think simple, like someone who is hearing it for the first time, because they are!

- **Think Visually.** Help your audience "see" what you say. This is the original idea behind using the PowerPoint software for presentations: say "dog," see "dog." The two go hand-in-hand. But more often, people build PowerPoint slides with a lot of verbiage on them and then read them. If this sounds familiar, rethink your design options.[20] Your audience knows how to read. Start planning your visuals in the outline. If you have anything complex, find ways to keep their attention with pictures. Many people are visual learners. If your presentation is longer than 15 minutes, you just might need visual stimulation.

- **Handouts.** While often quite useful, these should be used judiciously. They are intended to *support* your message, so providing a handout and then reading it is not only ineffective (dull, boring), it diverts attention away from you to a piece of paper. Most of your audience will read what is put in front of them the minute it is handed out so you might want to hold off distributing until it is needed or at the end of a meeting as a take-away.[21]

- **Use Touch and Smell when possible.** Let's take that car for a test drive! And remember the pie? Imagine being able to taste and smell it. Sold! Think outside the box. Let the product speak for you.

- **Interactive Activities.** Any presentation that requires people to move or interact makes a stronger

---

[20] Slideshare (slideshare.net) is a wonderful internet site dedicated to visually powerful and dynamics presentations.

[21] One of my personal pet peeves is receiving a handout only to be told to *not* look at it. Really? This rarely works anyway. And I do not advise letting your audience know at the beginning that you have a handout for them and so they don't need to take notes. This is basically giving them permission to not listen either.

impression than ones where they only sit and listen. Most people learn best by doing or seeing, and you will have a greater response when participants must be responsible to others in the group.

- **Questions from the Audience.** First, a brief word about waiting to ask for questions at the end of a presentation: Ugh!

How's that for brief? As I mentioned, I've sat through some pretty terrific (and not) presentations only to hear them end with a flat, "Any questions?" This is often followed by an uncomfortable silence. This person has poured their heart and soul into a presentation and no one can remember the question they had 20 minutes ago. The speaker then slinks away with something like, "OK, if there are no questions, that's about it; that's all I have to say... Thanks, everybody." Next!

Solutions: Ask for questions periodically and prompt *specific* questions: "I realize this new system may seem a little daunting so let's make sure we are clear before I proceed. Does anyone have any questions about the Command button?" Even if there is not a question specifically about the Command button, people are more likely to jump in with whatever is on their minds. This keeps a presentation lively and interactive.

Make it clear in your opening that questions are allowed. For some talks, questions simply aren't possible, but anytime a speech can seem more like a conversation... Bravo!

You may still ask for questions at the end, but make it a part of your prepared closing statement. Do not be a victim of a tragic ending where you, uh, drift off...

Practice Makes Pretty Good

Yes, I believe in practice, but if you look at the pie chart, I'm a realist. I know you are busy. I'm not suggesting that all, or even the majority of preparation time, be allotted to rehearsal. But at some point, it is time to stop writing, tweaking, finessing and massaging.

Find a room[22], ask for privacy and get up on your feet. Work with your visual aids.[23] Use the time to put your voice, face, eyes, hands and body into it. Your audience (and you) will be glad you did.

In closing this chapter and in the spirit of pie charts, let's bake an apple pie.

---

[22] If possible, find a space that is close in size to where you will be speaking.

[23] The first time you open that box and demonstrate a product should not be in front of an audience, unless you are hoping to make it on YouTube.

Hang in here with me. It sounds simplistic, but there are as many versions of apple pie as there are pages in this book and the influencing factors are numerous.

Using the ideas of ideal outcome and audience benefit, here is the scenario. You are bringing a homemade pie to your fiancé's parents' home, where you will meet them for the first time.

Here are two possibilities:

Pie #1: You are not a skilled baker but you've spent some time at the stove. How long could a pie take? You wait until the last minute, run to the corner quick-mart, and buy a frozen pie crust and a can of filling. Presto! Put them together, hopefully in the right order, place it in the oven (oops, you forgot to preheat, but that's OK, it'll get there eventually) and, yes, you have a pie and you made it!

Pie #2: Wanting to make a good impression, you shop for apples, butter, sugar, cinnamon and, yes, a frozen pie crust, because they are so darn good these days, no one can tell the difference. At home, you follow a recipe and wash the apples, then core, peel and slice them. The pie crust has been removed from the foil pan and placed into the glass one given to you by your Aunt Millie. (We love her!) You lay out the apples in a symmetrical design and cover them with little squares of butter. You liberally sprinkle this with sugar and cinnamon, flour and maybe a little nutmeg (also a tip from your Aunt). With the additional pie crust (they are typically sold in pairs) you cut the other one into strips and place these on the top in a crisscross pattern.

You place this masterpiece into the pre-heated 350°F oven and set the timer for 30 minutes, at which point you check to see if it is golden brown. Voilà!

Which one are you proud to present? If you don't care about baking and feel like an idiot in the kitchen (in which case, you should never have promised to bake something in the first place), you may want to order a deep dish in advance from that fantastic bakery everyone talks about. When you don't plan your time well or simply don't care, you buy the week-old pie at the grocery for $1.99. Even when it's just a pie, you get what you *plan* for. The key word is "plan."

Chapter 7.   Comfort vs. Objectivity

Still with me? We've addressed communication options and presentation structure. You have taken a deeper, but hopefully gentle, look at yourself, and perhaps you've gained a touch more objectivity in the way you view yourself and your situation.

How do you use any of these ideas to return to a more genuine, authentic self (opening your presence) *when some of this feels so strange?*

Perhaps you've dipped your toe in a new and improved presentation pool and... Brrr! You don't want to do that again! You wonder if you will ever feel truly comfortable again. You also want to know when. You want a guarantee that stepping out of that comfort zone will lead you to a better one. And you want it now.

Anything new is different and trying anything different requires an adjustment period. Period.

Mastering any new skill, whether it is baiting a hook, that painful pretzel pose in yoga class, golf, surgery or typing, means a learning curve and the level of discomfort is influenced by many factors from personal desire, time investment, complexity of the skill, familiarity, dexterity and possibly the competence of your teacher. Often the student is not able to appreciate the additional benefits nor future emotional satisfaction because it is not a part of the package.

The art of fishing provides lessons in patience, quiet and stillness.

Golf taught me the value of honesty and courtesy, and all of those hours on the course with my Dad proved to be a foundation for our lifelong bond.

I have learned so much about human nature from my clients that I think that will be the theme of my next book.

Embracing your power as a communicator has added benefits and I can't tell you what they will be. You will find them for yourself, if you are open and receptive to all that is provided.

A client confessed that he had no idea there was more to good presentation skills than learning to "memorize better." His increased eloquence and confidence has led to prestigious assignments and a promotion, but apart from work, his ability to publicly articulate his ideas helped him crystallize and act upon personal goals as well.

After improving her on-air delivery skills, an anchor client was offered a promotion to the evening news. She told me that when faced with the reality of the position she had worked for so fiercely, she was able to weigh the demands it would make on her family with the prestige and monetary benefits. She declined the promotion, but negotiated with management for a health reporter position. (This was considered a major step backward.) She said, "The main anchor position is what we all work for, but I realized my real passion is health and fitness. That includes a well-rounded life and now I have that."

One more story.

In his younger years, a very successful gentleman had been talked out of pursuing a television career by his father. He had gone into the family business as was expected. He was extremely successful, but came to me at his wife's urging to explore the possibilities of re-directing his career path.

We worked for several months and he was excellent; in many ways, a natural. When he was ready to meet with a television station and submit the sample reel we had produced, to my surprise, he pulled the plug. "You know, I think I just wanted to know if someone in the industry believed I had what it takes. Now I can embrace everything I've learned into my family business and do it with a better attitude."

Opening Your Presence

I tell you these stories to encourage you to keep going in your performance skills and push past the discomfort, while staying open to the many benefits of embracing and presenting your presence.

You may not fully understand who that is or what that means. A client admitted recently that she didn't even know what "being herself" meant because of all the hats she wore between home and her professional responsibilities as a business owner. She often felt conflicted as she put on the different "masks" each role demanded.

Another client told me that the need to always "hold it together," both professionally and personally, led him to use intimidation as a means of hiding his uncertainty. So much so that he rarely asked for help or guidance, even when it was appropriate to do so.

On the professional road to recognition, many people lose sight of their uniqueness and the power it plays in the journey to excellence. The clearest example of this is in the job interview, where the desire to prove worth supersedes presence. One may fixate so much on fitting the job mold that he finds himself in a revolving door of indecision and artificiality, projecting a false sense of self in an attempt to do what's right.

Let me be clear. There is a difference between "right" and "normal," and I want us to be on the same page with our verbiage.

"Normal" means what is typical or routine. If what is normal does not work, then it is not "right." There is no one right way to do something.

In this conversation, "right" is what is right for you, what is most productive and conducive to success, for both parties. This is a win-win. Remember?

Doing what is right for you, keeps in mind the other party.

We can thank Albert Einstein for defining insanity as "Doing the same thing over and over again and expecting different results."

If you picked up this book wanting different results, you've got to try something new. And *anything* new, in front of an audience, is simply not going to seem normal, "right" or comfortable, especially the first time. If you remain too entrenched in the comfort zone you may never know all that you are capable of.

In time, with a bit of practice and conscious application, you will eventually learn to rely on your instincts, which have been strengthened by practice and objectivity.

Just how do you determine *presentation success* when comfort is a mirage in the distance?

I have a couple of suggestions, although I must warn you, none of them go hand-in-hand with immediate gratification. These ideas will serve you well in the long run.

Audience Response

Part One: In the Moment

Get a "feel" for responses as you go along. This means assessing the reactions of the *majority* of the people- and not that one person who is texting.[24]

Are people nodding and listening? Do people seem to laugh and respond? How are people sitting? Slumped down or sitting upright? Do their eyes move and respond to visual clues?

For you to gauge any of this, it is necessary that *you* be in the moment, make eye contact, observe and absorb. This may be too much in the beginning, but it is your ultimate goal.

When you are prepared and able to be in that moment, you can respond to the demands of your audience.

---

[24] You will rarely grab everyone's attention, so don't focus on one person if the majority seems engaged.

Part Two: Post-Op

Being able to gauge your audience's responses following the presentation depends greatly on *your* attention to audience benefit, ideal outcome and intention.

If you know what you want them to do, think and feel, then you have a measuring stick. If you requested an action or response, did it happen?

I have had more than one client tell me that they felt a presentation went quite well, they weren't nervous, they hit their points, etc., and yet the results were minimal. Their team did not follow through with the assignment or no one responded to the program.

This is a sure sign that the presentation was lacking in some way. If you do not get the results or responses you would like, you have some work to do.

Got Video?

One of the best ways to gain valuable perspective is to video record your presentation, when possible. In this age of super phones and gadgets that do everything but clean your son's room, this should be fairly easy.

Here's the deal. You then have to watch it.

"You mean I have to *watch* myself?"

Yes, but I'm going to help you. Here are five key elements to watching a video so that the process is instructional and least painful:

1. Do *not* watch the video immediately following the presentation. Allow time for the emotional high or low to pass. I highly recommend a week or so. That high or low will greatly skew your perspective.

2. When you choose to watch your video, especially the first time (yes, you may even want to see it more than once), do so in private. Do it where you cannot be distracted, interrupted or embarrassed by anyone else. Decide for yourself how something came across as opposed to how it felt in the moment.

3. Begin with the sound muted so you can focus solely on the visual aspects of your delivery: facial expressions, eye contact and body language. Do you look connected to your audience? Are you physically engaged and engaging? What are you doing with your hands? Take your time and note what seems to be working and what doesn't. Remember that long pause where you couldn't think? Can you see it?

4. Now it's time to listen. Rewind, turn up the sound and watch this same section with your eyes closed. Listen to the elements of voice. Do you sound connected to the emotion and thought behind the words? How is your articulation and emphasis?

5. You may then rewind, open your eyes and watch the entire composition. Compare your observations to what you remember feeling at the time. Almost everyone finds discrepancies between how they felt in the moment and what they observe later. This is also a great time to check your toolbox and observe how you are utilizing (or not) the hands, face, body, eyes and voice. Check the "A" pyramid and make note of your appearance, actions, audio, attitude and audience.

The bottom line of this appraisal is to be specific and objective.

Alright! We have examined your dirty filters and smudged mirrors, we have talked about the five factors that affect how we form, send and receive messages, and we've looked inside your tool box. I've provided some guidelines for packaging your presentation product and how all the above requires attention, time and practice so that you may experience a legitimate and beneficial level of comfort. What now?

Chapter 8. What Do I Do Now?

Martha Stewart did not become "Martha Stewart" in a day and Warren Buffet did not become the investment genius he is with one stock trade. I'm sure Meryl Streep cringes at the thought of her first stab at acting and Alex Rodriguez, the youngest baseball player to hit 500 home runs, practiced that swing millions of times to cultivate his rhythm and style.

You will not hit the presentation jackpot in one pull either.

If you're anything like me, there is often that moment when I come to the end of a lesson or instructional book when I think, "What do I do now?" How do I keep going or take this to another level?

In my experience, I find that true growth follows revelations that are preceded by light bulb moments that come on the heel of small steps.

Movies have led us astray by the hero having that one big light bulb moment and then poof! He is a changed man. He lives happily ever after. The end.

In real life we have that light bulb moment after putting our finger in the socket. Oh, there may be a "Pow!" But it is not the end of the struggle. It is the beginning of a different battle.

*The development of your communication skills
is in direct proportion to the time and attention you give it.*

I urge you to keep taking the small steps that seem to make little impact, but in actuality reinforce the diving platform from which you take your greatest leap.

Take a step. And then take another. Take two. They're small.

Below are some bite-sized suggestions for continuing on the path to opening your presence.

Size Does Matter... So Start Small

Consumer debt counselors advise their clients to eliminate the smallest credit card debt first. If you have five credit cards, with balances ranging from $500 – $8,000, you are advised to eliminate the $500 balance first, while doing minimum maintenance on the rest to protect your credit rating.

This conflicts with a natural inclination to tackle the biggest debt, but there is sound reasoning here. In a shorter period of time, you have made a small, but significant, victory that creates a sense of accomplishment and one item gets scratched off the To Do list. Anything is possible!

The same principle is true when tackling performance skills. Start with one small task that provides a boost to your confidence, laying the groundwork for bigger and better.

Lance engaged my services because a recent promotion meant he was to speak at a large, company event. He was inexperienced in public speaking; even addressing co-workers in office meetings made him a bit nervous.

Luckily, we had a few months to prepare, so I suggested we start in the conference room. In the next few meetings, Lance would push himself to offer short, informal remarks, rather than observe quietly as he preferred. Soon he made a 3-minute presentation to a select group. He moved on to larger meetings, gradually making concise reports to 20-25 people. Updates that he previously sent by email, he offered as live updates. He then volunteered to speak to a group of about 100.

With each experience Lance's confidence, and more importantly, his abilities grew. We began rehearsing for the company-wide event a few weeks out. On the big day, he literally bounded up on the stage to greet 650 people with a huge smile and spoke for 30 minutes. The reception was overwhelming. This entire process took almost four months, but it started in a conference room.

He is now called on to speak to groups of all sizes regularly and he not only enjoys it, he welcomes the opportunity.

There are all kinds of circumstances that provide a platform on which to rehearse for the main event. I'm fortunate to live in a city where daily interactions are commonplace because public transit and walking are standard, but regardless of where you live, you must stop at the store, the coffee shop, the dry cleaner or the barber. They provide the practice in a (mostly) non-threatening environment.

After several small conquests, you will be ready to bring these skills into a larger playing field.

To Memorize or Not to Memorize?
It's Not Even a Question.

I once attended an awards dinner and the entertainment was a Master Memorizer. This guy was amazing. Audience members would call out all kinds of objects and lists and he could recite them backwards and forwards. It was impressive.

At the end of his program he began to thank his host. You know, the person who hired him and wrote his paycheck? Well, the Master Memorizer went blank! He could not remember the name of the company or person who had hired him.

For a moment I thought it was part of the act, but he was so flummoxed he couldn't bluff his way out of it. He literally stumbled around on the stage, took a shot and did *not* say the correct name.

He finally gave up and admitted that he could not remember. He was mortified and I was mortified for him.

I can recall very little of his presentation except that 10 years later I know that all those mental hijinks wouldn't do him one bit of good if he couldn't recall the name of his employer.

If this man couldn't memorize a name and recall it under pressure, imagine what is in store for the rest of us.

Memorizing a speech perfectly and regurgitating it word-for-word doesn't benefit you or the audience if you do not convey the essence and passion behind the words.

I've had more than one person tell me they just try to memorize a presentation so they can't mess up or stumble. Hah! Very few people can effectively memorize a two-minute speech much less one that is 20 – 30 minutes. Then throw in any kind of disruption, like a question or a technical issue? Please! This is a recipe for disaster.

In the long run, speaking by rote probably leads to *more* stumbles.

If you buy into little else of what I say, I hope you accept the wisdom that *how* you say something is more powerful, more meaningful and typically more memorable than *what* exact words you choose. Memorization does not get you there.

Commit to memorize less and speak from knowledge. Take every minute that you might spend memorizing and invest that time in being of service to your audience. Embrace your purpose and intention, prepare and rehearse, then reap the benefits.

Know Your Opening

I know, I know... I've already talked about this, but I have a good reason for repeating it.

I stress the idea of "knowing your opening" to every client for whom it is applicable.

When in rehearsal, I ask for their opening and I am told, "Well, I thought I'd start with my name and say something about their new quota and my expectations for their performance in the new product roll-out..."

Aarrgghh! I know that we are having our own communication glitch.

To know your opening does not mean that you have a vague sense of how you might want to begin. I mean *know* the words, the sentiment, the purpose and intention behind those words.

This is as close as I ever come to encouraging memorization, so take me up on it. Embrace the freedom this knowledge gives you to be flexible in the moment.

I was in the audience as a speaker (not my client) approached the stage in such a distracted state that his lips were actually moving. I think he was still rehearsing.

Just then, a chipmunk ran up on the stage, passing so close to him it looked like he would step on the scene stealer. Some of the audience near the front gasped, people laughed and whispered.

Everyone responded, except the speaker. He was oblivious. He was so consumed with his notes and what lay ahead, he was sleepwalking.

Imagine if this gentleman had been prepared, sure of his opening so that he could think on his feet. He might have improvised something funny, "I haven't even started and already my audience is running for the door," or at least laughed along with everyone else.

Eliminating unnecessary distractions frees up the brain to think and sometimes literally "see" the options before you.

A skilled surgeon can improvise in an emergency only when he is aware of all of his options.

Can you imagine feeling so liberated as to go with the flow in a presentation? If so, bravo. If not, it is possible.

Having a great opening statement (and, yes, it is helpful to think it is great) is a step in that direction. You show respect to your audience when you care enough to be prepared.

This is one of the easiest small steps to take. No one will ever know that this seemingly random thought so excellently expressed in the moment was actually well thought-out and planned.

Pick an "A," Any "A"

When you're feeling stuck and you don't know what to do to invigorate your speeches, grab one of those five As from Chapter 4 and chew on it.

To improve your performance skills you must be mindful and nothing makes us more mindful than a long look in the mirror.

Appearance is a great place to start. Styles change. Our responsibilities grow. Titles and positions are reassigned. Does your appearance send the right message?

If not, you have a myriad of options for experimentation. Get a stylist. Ask an expert. Hire a personal shopper. Go to the barber or the hairdresser. Just stop doing the same thing because it looked so good in college.

Rejuvenation of one's appearance offers inspiration to the mind and spirit.

Move on to another "A" and another experiment. Push boundaries.

Make an Attitude Adjustment

When you find yourself struggling, caught up in a web of details and conflict, take a step back and analyze the attitude that may be skewing your perspective.

Let's say that an upcoming project (or even a necessary conversation) fills you with dread. The chances of a fantastic outcome are small.

Adjusting your attitude does not mean you become filled with joy and force yourself to dance with glee at the prospect. However, it works to your favor to examine the source of your anxiety and shift your focus. Make a list. Look for ways to refocus your attention by digging deep into intention and ideal outcome and what it will take to get there.

Create a brief mission statement or mantra to help align focus and actions. Your mission statement is personal and should "feel" right for you and no one else. They should be short, positive and *not shared with others*.[25]

---

[25] Mission statements are powerful tools used by highly successful individuals and corporations across the globe. There are a multitude of resources and authorities on mission statements, but I personally

I am not suggesting you walk around sounding like Stuart Smalley, with his "I'm good enough, I'm smart enough, and doggone it, people like me!"[26] (Bless his heart.) But the idea is correct.

We all have silent monologues playing out in our minds. There is no Stop button on this player. You have to change the CD or at least buy some new iTunes. Why not *replace* negative, destructive discourses with something positive and beneficial?

I love that Ellen DeGeneres encourages her guests and audience members to dance on her show. Thoughts and mood are highly responsive to sound and physical movement.

I work with a team, who breaks up Friday afternoon slumps with music and a quick dance around the office. This is a form of reprogramming and it's less fattening than cookies.

I have found that most of my clients with great outlooks are very conscious of their mindset. They *know* they are being positive.

---

appreciate Stephen R. Covey's thoughts in *The 7 Habits of Highly Effective People*.

[26] Stuart Smalley, created and performed by Al Franken, was a character seen on Saturday Night Live in the early '90s. If you haven't seen any of these comedy bits, it's worth an internet search.

On the other hand, negativity sneaks up on us. I've often come into contact with people who didn't realize how negative they were or felt they were powerless to be otherwise.

Your attitude is in sync with your internal monologue. That voice reflects your attitude, and attitude feeds upon the monologue. They are affected by a variety of external influences and it is up to you to participate in the program selection.

Remember you always have choices. Attitude is a choice that can and should be made, for if you do not do so consciously, one is imposed on you.

Improvisation is Not Just for Comedy Anymore

I suggest that you run, do not walk, to your local comedy club. Why? Because this is where improvisation classes are usually found.

I am frequently asked if there are additional classes I recommend and improvisation is it. Comedy shows may make it look easy, but there is real skill and principles behind improvisation that serve the business professional well. Improvisation has guidelines that provide structure to the skit, such as being in the moment, relating to the other person, building on opportunities, and solving problems.

The first rule of improv is to say "yes" and agree, because now there is a foundation on which to build. Believe it or not, the first rule of improv is *not* "Thou must be funny at all costs."

I've seen powerful, seemingly unplanned professional successes arise from adherence to the principles of improvisation. Basic, introductory skills provide a strong basis for thinking on one's feet, being able to respond in the moment, and speaking with confidence in multiple settings and situations. It's a win-win scenario and, by the way, you laugh too.

I am always asked about Toastmasters© and for the record I want to say that I see great value in associations like this. It offers a platform for some of the practice, practice, practice I believe is so important.

The downside I've observed is getting inadequate feedback from other, equally inexperienced attendees. One of the first premises I offer in Chapter 1 is "consider the source." Done with the right attitude, Toastmasters and similar organizations are useful resources, but should be thought of as one ingredient in a bigger pie, not the complete recipe for success.

Imitation is the Highest Form of Flattery...
Or is It?

I find that understanding why someone does something is more interesting and enlightening than what exactly they are doing. Actors often spend months or weeks during the rehearsal process getting to the bottom of what motivates a character's actions.

In business I've witnessed a lot less reflection and a lot more imitating. It seems to reason that if Mr. X is doing it and Mr. X has more experience and a bigger title, then it must be right.

But imitation without reflection can lead to a whole lot of bad imitating.

> It is not all that unusual for on-air anchors to operate their own teleprompter via a computer mouse or a foot pedal, much like one on a sewing machine.
>
> At a client station, I noticed that all of the anchors seemed to have a funny tic, almost like a jerk in the shoulders, that seemed to be associated with operating the foot pedal.
>
> After working with a particularly energetic young man who seemed intent on stomping it into the floor, I logically deduced there must be a problem with the system. Possibly the pedal was sticky or needed maintenance, so I made an inquiry.
>
> No, the system was brand new. It was explained to me that it just worked that way. Hmmm... This sounded fishy to me,

so I tried it out for myself. With the barest whisper of a touch, the prompter script moved forward.

I did some investigating. As it turned out, a veteran of this station was responsible for teaching everyone how to operate the prompter. He had worked with the old system, which did have a sticky pedal. He was instructing everyone in the only way he knew and was passing along the very method that caused carpal tunnel in his foot!

No one had questioned his technique, nor had anyone noticed the tic I had found so distracting. Familiarity may not breed contempt, but it often leads to blindness.

This may seem like a ridiculous example, but I've seen mindless imitation come in many forms and every environment, from style of dress and manner of speech (vocal fry, anyone?) to building a PowerPoint slide deck.

I have heard, "But Mr. X does it!" from the same person who admits they don't like a particular technique or find it ineffective, yet are still inclined to follow the pack.[27]

I do not advocate imitating, but I highly recommend emulating. This requires being observant and mindful of the essence to a person's style, so that you may embrace the spirit without imitating falsely. It also reduces the erroneous belief that this other person is right and therefore, you must be wrong.

---

[27] This is not to be confused with following office procedure.

Give some thought to the motivation behind seemingly simple actions that may not be serving you well.

Imitation requires little energy and no imagination. It is not authentic.

Emulation is fueled by purpose, requires thoughtful observation, and can be modified to the individual.

Too Many Cooks

"Too many cooks spoil the broth" and too many opinions confuse the presenter. Ask 14 people what they think and you will likely get 14 contrasting viewpoints. You may be seeking help to make a decision or even hope to substantiate the choice you've made, but you are more likely to wind up exasperated.

There is a big difference between seeking constructive instruction and gathering evidence for verification.

A client sought her husband's input numerous times a day on a variety of subjects. She often came into our sessions to tell me what he had said and what he thought, but she struggled to verbalize her own. One day she actually stopped our session to call her husband to ask his opinion. I knew they spoke frequently, but I was surprised by this sudden interruption. When she hung up I asked her how often they spoke during the day. Her quick answer was a couple, then a few, and after discussion she admitted they spoke upward of a dozen times daily, although both were employed in fulltime positions.

I then understood why she struggled to express herself. She wasn't allowing time to form her own opinion before seeking the guidance of someone else.

The four aspects to examine when garnering advice are:

- How many
- How often
- Who
- When

How many people are you asking and why? This often goes hand in hand with **how often**, because you aren't hearing what you want to hear so you expand the circle hoping to get the "right" answer!

Understanding **who** you ask is enlightening. As with my client who always sought her husband's guidance, she trusted his opinion over her own. I understood her initial inclination as he worked in a similar industry and had far more experience and seniority. But she was missing the opportunity to develop her instincts.

Like the parent who completes the child's homework for him, the desire behind the action may be well-meaning ("I just wanted to help"), but the action defeats the purpose.

When you ask for input is important because of the way it may impede (or nurture) the quality of the input.

It is not the best time to seek opinions in a group. A personal friend who may feel comfortable offering guidance or instruction may be hesitant or "edit" his or her comments in front of others.

You may also want to wait if your emotions are extremely high or low, is not the time to seek input.

Does this sound familiar?

> *I can't believe I lost my place! I went absolutely blank for at least 5 minutes! It felt like 5 minutes. Was it 5 minutes? Could you tell? How long was it? Was it forever? Did I look panicked? I must have looked like an insane person... Blah, blah, blah...*

What do you *think* people are going to say? "Actually it was 7 minutes. I timed you and it was awful. You poor thing!"

People will most likely tell you exactly what you need to hear at that moment, "It was fine! I hardly noticed!"

This may or may not be true, but chances are you will not believe them. So you ask again and again. And you still don't believe them, but maybe you feel a little better. Most likely, you do not.

Likewise, you don't want to ruin a perfectly legitimate presentation by being too high as you step off the platform.

Opening Your Presence

> *Oh my goodness, I can't believe how well that went! I knocked it out of the park! Wow! I'm so happy! I really didn't think I could do it, but I did, didn't I? Didn't I?*

No one would want to ruin your moment by telling you that your microphone was cutting out and the blue light shining on your face made you look like a Smurf. (This actually happened to me, by the way!)

The way to receive useful input is to understand your motivation. Know what you seek to learn and why. I applaud the idea of asking for help. We all need it from time to time. A nudge in the right direction is no more than a click away. It is the job of the professional consultant to be objective, constructive and help you find solutions.

My opinions are educated opinions, not based on personal likes or dislikes. I do not expect clients to blindly receive *everything* I say, but I do expect them to be open to new concepts. One of those is "Stop asking everyone what they think!"

In the event you do not or cannot hire a coach, seek guidance from *one* trusted source, ideally not an immediate family member, your boss or someone who reports to you. These people may find it difficult to be completely honest, no matter how much you insist. Worse yet, if they speak honestly and you do not like or agree with what they have to say, you are asking for hurt feelings. Seek input judiciously. And hopefully, not as you walk away from the podium.

See the Good, the Bad and the Ugly...
And I Don't Mean the Movie

The best chance you have of opening your presence is to acknowledge *all* of your presents: the good, the bad and the ugly.

We don't love every gift we receive, but hopefully we receive graciously. We might exchange, re-gift or perhaps in time, appreciate what we didn't or couldn't before.

We find that even if we never grow to love it, we may value the thought behind the gift or the giver. So your Aunt Millie has bad taste. She serves you well in other ways.

I believe it is essential to recognize all of our presentation gifts. Know what works, what is strong and good, so that you may use it again and again. Accept the ugly because, chances are, the "ugly" is not as ugly as you once thought.

I recently conducted a workshop where a young lady heard her voice for what she swore was the first time. She said she had hated her voice her whole life and just couldn't listen to it.

All workshop participants were required to participate in our video-recorded activities and she asked that we watch her playback in private. We started with the sound off. I then asked her to close her eyes and listen. She was amazed at what she heard. When I asked her to describe her voice she said, "That's amazing! I have gone all of this time thinking my voice was so high and squeaky. It is really a bit low, isn't it?"

Yes, it was.

I have come to recognize that it is not the truth some clients fear, but just the opposite. A gentleman told me he assumed the compliment was a lie, an assuagement to lessen the blow. ("Come on, Doc. Give it to me straight… How long do I have?")

In the movie "Pretty Woman," Julia Roberts' character Vivian tells the Richard Gere character that "the bad stuff is easier to believe." This falls in line with the Brené Brown theory I mentioned earlier. Most people define things by what they are not.

For whatever reason, I've worked with many people who can't accept the good, but eat up the bad with a spoon. These clients want to *fix what is wrong!*

I understand that. But sometimes the best solution is to take the focus off the imperfection and allow one's strength to supersede.

The first step is to accept everything as it is. *All* of it.

> *Acceptance of a strength makes it stronger.*
>
> *Acceptance of a challenge diminishes it.*
>
> *Acceptance of the whole allows for*
> *creative problem-solving.*

Working with a perceived flaw or limitation (either personally or professionally) is like a blemish. Picking at it makes it worse. Staring and obsessing makes it *seem* worse. Ignore it and it might go away... eventually.

With proper treatment, it heals. The bad is only as bad as we think it is. The ugly is primarily in our minds.

This section wouldn't be complete without addressing one particular challenge in embracing one's strengths. I've interacted with a great number of people who believe that to acknowledge their strengths would seem rude or egotistical.

The kind of acceptance I am talking about could not be farther from the arrogance associated with an inflated sense of superiority. Embracing one's ability to make others laugh is not the same as believing you are the funniest person in the room. Appreciating one's voice, charm, prettiness or grace allows for greater expression of each.

With attention to what *is* you find balance.

To use your tools properly, you must understand and value their qualities. This provides the foundation for objectivity and appreciation for all that you have and all that you are.

In Closing

Being able to express and reveal the essence of oneself requires courage and persistence. I hope the stories and simple methodology here have provided opportunities for experiencing a more meaningful exploration of your talents and assures you that you are not alone in your struggle to find your authentic voice.

Have you ever heard something, it could have been on the evening news, overheard in a restaurant, around the proverbial water cooler or, yes, even on Oprah and Ding! Ding! Ding! The bell goes off and you think, *"That is the truest thing I've ever heard!"*

If you didn't know better, you'd think it was the first time you ever heard it. But you know, you have heard it before, possibly only within yourself, and *you* know it to be true.

When you have those light bulb moments, go to the light. Run, walk or mosey, but explore what you believe to be true or right for you.

The secret is to establish a strong connection with that instinct and renew your trust in yourself.

Your genuine self is the present waiting to be opened.

Enjoy your presents and may you accept *all* the gifts that create your presence.

Best Wishes,

Acknowledgements

It takes two to tango and a village to raise a child. This project has benefited from countless people who shared their stories, expertise, challenges and encouragement. I would like to do a few special shout-outs as there are too many for adequate billing.

In the past six years, I have collaborated with two very talented colleagues through a deliciously liberating partnership at C3 Coaching Concepts and Consulting (c3nyc.com). Amy Griggs Kliger and Lee Ritchey have offered encouragement while serving as co-consultants, sounding boards, coaches and, most importantly, good friends. On many occasions Amy and her husband, Jack Kliger, graciously allowed me to  use their home in Sag Harbor as a writing retreat where much of this book evolved. They also provided Sammy, their bulldog, for company who often broke a creative slump. How could he not with that face?

Lee used his sharp wit and creative collaboration to inspire the phrase, "Open Your Presence," which I have been using as a theme for my workshops since 2010. Thank you.

My illustrator is a talented artist and teacher in New Jersey (eyegateart.com) and she is also my sister. Roberta Muller Granzen has believed in me and encouraged me for as long as I can remember and I am honored to have her artwork grace these pages.

The animated videos on our C3 website (c3nyc.com) were designed and executed by the talented Eryn Rieple. Lyndsey Rieple is a gifted jewelry designer by profession, but she is a natural coach and inspiration, who rarely lets a week go by without checking on me. I love and thank both of these young ladies who I am proud to say call me "Aunt Greta."

David O'Bryan slugged through an early draft of this book and offered encouragement and insights that helped me focus my intention. Thank you.

I sincerely thank Chris Westfall and Tara Alemany who helped bring this book to the printed page and digital realm.

I wish I had room to go into more detail, but I hope I have articulated my appreciation individually so that these people understand the depth of my gratitude for all they have done for me: Don Piper, Charles Gremillion, Lorna Allen, Talene Staab, Beverly Edwards, Betty Rothbart, Rick Janecek, Don Kinnison, Donna and Benny DiChiara,

Anthony LaMattina, Melinda Barnes, Tanya Troyer, Shari Porter Jung, my beautiful Lunch Bunch of Dallas (Ethel, Lou, Nancy, Andrea and Angie), the glorious Lit Chicks of New York (Teresa, Robin, Leslie A, Leslie G, Marcia, Dianne and Christina), and of course, my clients, who inspire and teach me every day.